Education at the Crossroads

New Thoughts of the Changing Era

Education at the Crossroads

New Thoughts of the Changing Era

Editor

Dr. Amitabh Roy

AUTHORSPRESS

Worldwide Circulation through Authorspress Global Network
First Published in 2020
by
Authorspress
Q-2A Haus Khas Enclave, New Delhi-110 016 (India)
Phone: (0) 9818049852
E-mail: authorspressgroup@gmail.com
Website: www.authorspressbooks.com

Education at the Crossroads:
New Thoughts of the Changing Era
ISBN 978-93-90459-79-7

Printed in India at Thomson Press (India) Limited

Acknowledgement

I am extremely thankful to all the contributors for sharing their thoughts through their research articles. These articles have addressed various issues – issues which are presently not only of national importance but also internationally significant. I express my heartfelt gratitude to the contributors for expressing their concern and also trying to think of probable solutions.

Dr. Amitabh Roy

Preface

The hybridity of educational world is reflected well during the happenings worldwide for past few months. We are talking of a time which is suddenly rife with alternative ways of dissemination of knowledge broadening the horison of traditional classroom teaching. We are at a point of transition for which we had started dreaming but were hesitant about its ways of adoption. Pandemic is not the only cause of the shift from traditional limited teaching options to unlimited opportunity of digital distribution. Rather, a hybrid approach is necessary in this age of globalisation to make the whole world a small classroom.

Education, be it primary or higher studies, cannot be kept confined within a small periphery. The blessings of digital dissemination of classroom teaching can do wonders. However, at the same time it can also bring to fore the question of class division. The so called 'digital divide' is also to be focused upon.

In this collection of 22 essays, we have sincerely tried to look into such pluralities with an open mind. Naturally, we have essays ranging from discussion of new possibilities of teaching during the pandemic to the novel idea of setting up digital universities. The issue of mental health as well as the barriers faced by the students are discussed with analytical approach.

2020 is a year with such long lasting wounds that we cannot forget easily. The education sector, though primarily thought to be in a spell, soon came back with innumerable ways to keep the wheel moving. The force behind such unhindered movement is nothing but the spirit, that lies within education itself. At present, we are at the crossroads in the truest sense of the term. We are at that juncture from where we have to embrace new thoughts of this changing era. With a high speed broadband connection, the farthest corner of a village will be able to receive education from faculty at Harvard. The blessings of digital opportunities cannot be kept in abeyance, rather it is explored and materialised.

Policy planning should be an alternative to the facts that we cannot avoid any more. It is the call of time that facility of digitisation should be made a fundamental right every student. A student living in the rural area should not be deprived of broadband and must enjoy the same educational facilities as students residing in urban area. Issues crop up and soon disappear. But, educational opportunities are not mere 'issues'; they are our pillars of societal development and mental well-being.

Dr. Amitabh Roy

Contents

1

Lesions and Lessons: Education and the Pandemic

Abhishek Das

Introduction

Adversities have often proven to be the advertisements for resilience and tenacity of civilisations over time and space. The ability to re-mould and re-model when faced with challenges has allowed continuance and prosperity of the human race and the recent pandemic to have afflicted the globe seems to be a similar event to attest and affirm the Promethean spirit that lies at the core of human existence. These are unprecedented times and unprecedented have been the responses to address the threat. As the novel virus has successfully altered the conceptualisation of 'normative' across the individual and social spectrum, a cult of innovation, albeit driven primarily by the rhetoric of technology, has gained traction. It is vis-à-vis this scenario, that as an educationist it is important to probe the dominant rhetoric of the 'new normal' and its ever expanding clique of ardent backers.

It is almost a foregone conclusion that the pandemic has proven to be a catalyst in overhauling the existent pattern of knowledge dissemination. The erstwhile 'whisper' that pervaded the academia regarding the fear of technology supplanting the brick and mortar classrooms, across the globe has now become a deafening clamor. The antiquated classroom lecture method with its associated set of entrenched institutional biases and apathy has suddenly found its nemesis in the smart platforms, promoted and peddled aggressively, primarily by Ed-tech companies and to some extent the government. With these profit making entities mushrooming all around, alluring their 'customers' with the promise of a more egalitarian and equitable access to education, at the click of a button, at their chosen moment of convenience, it seems like a losing battle for the traditional academicians. However, the intent is not to write an epigraph for this threatened group, but to look closely at 'teaching' as an extremely complex and extraordinary job whose ambit extends far beyond the here and now, the tangible and quantifiable realm of 'value' that is more often than not, perceived in monetary terms.

The purpose of education, one ought to realise, is not merely to stimulate the intellectual potential of an individual, but also to instil compassion and empathy in the recipients. Therefore, the task of the educator is not merely to enhance the epistemological quotient, but to ensure a humane and conducive value system in which it should be entrenched. In the operational execution front, this can only be warranted when learning can be presented, not merely with the semblance of verisimilitude, as promised by digital educational platforms, aided by technological tools, but by ensuring a direct human interface between the learner and the instructor. This is however not to be confused as a Luddite's dictum, but a fervent desire to maintain the quintessential humane ingredient, devoid of which, education will be diminished to the business of manufacturing 'cogs' for the monetised 'wheel'.

The situation triggered by COVID-19 has become a catalyst for educational institutions worldwide to put all or most of their eggs in the 'technological basket'. Traditional-in-person classroom teaching is gradually getting substituted by newer learning modalities. Podcasts, live broadcasts, educational influencers, augmented/virtual reality are terminologies that have invaded the hitherto mundane world of classroom learning. There is little doubt that students have been beneficiaries of these changes. The need to commute to attend lectures is no longer a compulsion for them. Similarly, they are allowed to study at the pace they desire and can utilise a quieter working environment for the same. It holds the promise of inculcating better time management skills making them more disciplined in the process. Even teachers can device innovative methods to check students' learning in this environment. Therefore, 'blended learning' for substantial transformation in curriculum development and pedagogy has gained increased acceptance. Another area that has received notable attention is the domain of collaborative efforts, global and otherwise, between faculty members as well as learners, further bolstering the dream of a global classroom. Along with these positive aspects, the students stand a chance at gaining extremely useful skills, such as IT, adaptability, and a greater sense of working within a digital space. There have been instances galore, where students have leveraged their newly acquired digital skills to open avenues of learning interfaces, hitherto unexplored.

It is also unarguably one of the most affordable options as compared to the offline mode of learning. This is an alluring prospect, particularly in a developing nation where resources available are woefully scarce. In a country like India, where a measly budgetary allocation is reserved for the education sector, possibility of massive reduction in institution cost must appear like the proverbial 'genie out of the lamp' for the decision makers at the top most echelons. Additionally, the proponents of a 'digital India' would gleefully clutch at this opportunity without fail, and might also parade the various government backed platforms such as *Diksha, e-pathshala, NROER, Swayam, Swayam Prabha* as tailor made portals to transform the education scenario in the country. Remote learning, undoubtedly, has captured the fancy of the planners and decision makers. In addition to this, the Online Disinhibition Effect, as pointed out by psychologist John Suler, wherein physical barriers to feeling empowered, such as age, race, gender and skin tone can be relatively relaxed online, allowing for a more authentic expression of self, can be considered as a major positive aspect. But, one must be equally aware of the flipside of this novel transformation.

The success of the 'remote learning' model is infinitely dependent on the presence of motivated teachers and learners, who ought to be knowledgeable about the technical paraphernalia associated with online platforms. Additionally, they should have access to superior internet facility to take advantage of this mode of knowledge dissemination. In a country like India, with siseable number of people forced to live a hand to mouth existence, and with a mere fifty percent internet penetration, fulfilling the basic requirements for the remote learning model to succeed is but a pauper's dream. Also, the possibility of ennui, creeping in the participants of online discussion sessions is bound to get farther aggravated with subsequent hurdles perpetuated by poor living standards. There have been newspaper reports of students and their guardians, choosing to end their lives, when they weren't able to buy gadgets to access online classes. With joblessness increasing at an alarming rate and the economy groaning under the strain caused by the pandemic, affording internet packs for the classes is a luxury that many can ill afford. Therefore, in a bid to democratise education, by encouraging extensive usage of the digital platforms, we must ask, if we are in effect distancing a siseable section of the most underprivileged population from accessing quality education. Also to be considered is the immediate lacunae in this remote learning module, whereby the learners often are left with a sense of compromised learning experience due to the absence of accountability. With no teacher available to address their myriad doubts instantly, there is a presumable delivery-gap that hampers the process of learning. A disruption in the familiar learning space, coupled with divided attention, owing to the constant need to fiddle with technological aspects of the platform, interrupts the psychological contract with the instructor.

Moreover, government run schools in India also double up as centers where the young and adolescent students are provided with a portion of their daily dietary requirement, through the Mid-Day Meal Scheme. These schools are often the only means of social contact among students from disparate classes and castes. The uncritical urge to embrace online platforms as a substitute for classroom learning model might lead the country to miss the forest for the trees. The remote learning model should be encouraged at the upper end of the educational taxonomy. At the primary and secondary school education level, more emphasis should be laid on classroom teaching, albeit with some avenues for introducing the students to measured digital exposure. Only at the graduate and post graduate level, a larger section of the curriculum should be allowed to be taught using digital tools, through digital mediums. The rationale behind this being that at an impressionable age, there are chances that the learners would be more prone to misuse of digital resources rather than using them analytically. Also, one needs to be reminded of the fact that unfettered access to digital modes can adversely affect their physical well-being. Constant exposure to computer screens will prove harmful for their eyes and continuous presence in a secluded space, with no human communication with peers from similar age groups, would restrict their socialising skills to a great degree. One must realise that classrooms facilitate learning of social skills in children and not merely academic accomplishments. Therefore, efforts must be made to ensure that students get to share a common physical space, and not merely meet each other in a virtual territory.

The need of the hour is to fashion a measured response to the altered scenario, brought about by the onslaught of the pandemic, and extract all that is good in the erstwhile system of classroom centered learning model, and supplement it with newer technological aids. In fact there is a scope for introducing the students to the benefit of using Radio as a means to bridge the technological chasm. Unlike internet based platforms, its reach is wider and it is decidedly cheaper, apart from it being extremely easy to use. Moreover, the Indian students have been long exposed to this technology. Indian radio has about a four-decade long history of working towards educational purposes. The Rural Radio Forum for Agricultural Development (1967), promotion of adult literacy rate and GRAMS experiment of 1975 have already tasted success. Similarly, Gyan Vani, an educational FM Radio network functioning through several FM stations, which was meant to operate with programmes contributed by different educational institutions, NGOs and national level institutions like IGNOU,

NCERT and UGC can be upgraded to aid the existing educational infrastructure. It will be fruitful to reiterate at this juncture, that the unequivocal call to merely substitute classrooms with digital platforms would merely be tantamount to throwing the baby out with the bathwater. In a country such as India, with mindboggling social, economical, and geographical diversities, planning and decision making, particularly in a sensitive sector such as education, the backbone of the nation, must involve a consideration for plurality of circumstances. An abrupt move towards rapid and unduly invasive digitalisation might very well be counter-productive.

However, it also must be stated without equivocation that change is the very essence of any structure that vies for lasting relevance. The responsibility of maintaining a feasible equilibrium between the old and the new systems therefore lie primarily with the educationists themselves. The teachers must realise the dynamic nature of their profession and adapt accordingly. Their profession enjoins upon them to be ethical, compassionate, inspirational and compassionate and not merely to be the repositories of discipline specific information. With search engines such as Google and Baidu ruling the roost, every novice can have information at their fingertip with just a click. A teacher therefore, must be a facilitator to ensure that the learners can involve themselves critically with the knowledge they gather. As an instructor and guide, one must be capable enough to instill analytical skills in the students thereby training them to use information in the most apt manner and not merely regurgitate them. Teachers have to be curators of information and encourage students to question, critique, synthesise and apply knowledge. Most importantly, they must inculcate humane values by being exemplars themselves. This is the quintessential virtue of real education that can be taught better in person, rather than in a Soom classroom or through a Google Meet platform.

Conclusion

It can be concluded by saying that on its part, the society must also realise that the real purpose of education is not to produce programmed automatons, but thinking individuals. Since the pandemic has further aggravated the move towards skill based education, aimed at providing suitable choice of vocations to the beneficiaries, the society must ensure the continuance of liberal arts and humanities to be taught with equal emphasis. The future generations must continue receiving education, with its core values kept intact. As the primary stakeholders, the teachers and learners must unite to ensure that the post-pandemic situation would leave in its wake a 'fairer-normal' and not merely a 'new-normal'.

References

Biswas, Atanu. (2020, September 14). "Take-Home exams the new normal." *The Statesman,* p.7.

Bhattacharjee, Govind. (2020, September 5). "Devil in the Details." *The Statesman,* p.6.

Department of Education (2020), Coronavirus (COVID 19): implementing protective measures in education and childcare settings, GOV.UK website.

Ganguly, Aryapriya. (2020, October 13). "Adding Diversity to Learning Styles." *The Statesman,* P.11.

Ghosh, A.K. (2020, August 24). "Covid and Radio." *The Statesman,* p.6.

.... (2020, September 7). "The Open Book Route." *The Statesman.* P.6

Gupta, Sachin. (2020, October 13). "Growing Familiarity with Digital World." *The Statesman,* p.11.

Ravitch, Diane. (2001). "Left Back: A Century of Battles Over School Reforms." *Touchstone.*

Rajput, Mayank. (2020). *Impact of Covid-19 on Education: 20 Effects on Schooling in India.* Independent Publishing.

Sarma, Sanjay & Yoquinto, Luke. (2020). *Grasp: The Science Transforming How We Learn.* Doubleday.

Skinner, B.F. (1974). *About Behaviorism.* Penguin Books.

Seymour, Papert. (1994). *The Children's Machine: Rethinking School in The Age Of The Computer.* Basic Books.

2

Rethinking of Knowledge Advancement & Pedagogy in the Post Covid-19 Era: From the Perspective of Curriculum Studies

Ajay Prakash Tiwari and **Dileep Kumar Maurya**

Introduction

Instructive frameworks are moreover getting ready for the post COVID-19 period portrayed by "new ordinary." This articulation previously rose in the field of business. It was utilised to alert the conviction of market analysts that modern economies would return to typical after the downturn (El-Erian, 2010). The term has since been utilised in various settings to imply that something which was already not run of the mill has gotten average. The Urban Dictionary (2009) depicted "new ordinary" as the circumstance of being after some serious change has happened. It substitutes the acknowledged, constant, regular state after a specific occasion occurred.

A few insightful works have been as of late distributed to handle the multidimensional ramifications of COVID-19 emergency to the normal new ordinary time frame (for example see Sintema, 2020a and Toquero, 2020 on instructive; Radwan and Radwan, 2020 on social and financial; Usak et al., 2020 on social and mental). Inside the instructive measurement, there has been broad investigates talking about the reception of online methodology in instructional usage in the new typical post-COVID-19 time (for example see Sintema, 2020b on digitalised virtual study hall; Basilaia and Kvavadse, 2020 on online training; Naciri et al., 2020 on versatile learning; Mulenga and Marbán, 2020 on advanced learning).

These developing conversations as respects training in the new typical post-COVID-19 period could be reexamined through the viewpoint of educational program examines. An educational program can be characterised as an arrangement that has components. In light of the original educational program advancement models (for example Tyler, 1949; Taba, 1962), these components of the educational program are the objective, substance, approach, and assessment. Drawing thoughts from this point of view, an educational program advancement considering the moving toward new ordinary post-COVID-19 period, a reexamining of training inside the educational program examines points of view is significant. It presents looks at circumstances and difficulties later on for training taking everything into account. By talking about the educational plan prospects as far as objective, substance, approach, and assessment, instructors in the field will be better educated regarding the key issues, choices, and arrangements that must be fittingly considered as we approach the new time.

Accordingly, this paper endeavored to reconsider training in the new ordinary post-COVID-19 time from the viewpoint of educational plan examines.

A Focus on Preparedness as a Goal

The new typical post-COVID-19 period opens an open door for reevaluating the objectives of instruction. One of the objectives to make the educational plan important, suitable, and responsive is the advancement of readiness in the midst of catastrophes, illnesses, and crises. There are existing educational program objectives that address a lot of readiness skills in the various fields of study. Nonetheless, the focal point of these objectives is explicitly on catastrophic event readiness. Considering the coming new typical post-COVID-19 period, there is a longing for a more centered objective around readiness as far as worldwide malady episodes.

While planning the objective of readiness, there is a need to characterise it. Nonetheless, apparently a concurred meaning of readiness is a test, for example, its present status in the clinical training (McCabe et al., 2010; Nelson et al., 2007). It appears to stay a dubious idea wherein its landscapes have not been characterised well. It is normal however to meet the related terms, for example, wellbeing readiness (Khan et al., 2018), crisis readiness (Gebbie and Qureshi, 2002), and calamity readiness (Kent, 1994).

There has been a call to incorporate readiness content into the educational program. Fundamental training schools have reasonably joined readiness structures in their educational plan as of late. In numerous nations like the Philippines, readiness as an objective of training for youthful students has been given consideration (Kagawa and Selby, 2014; Valencia et al., 2018). Be that as it may, as readiness is as yet a sloppy crossroads, it is obscure if readiness across various kinds of catastrophes, illnesses, and crises are the equivalent. It ought to be noticed that in the new ordinary post-COVID-19 period, there is a need to contextualise such readiness objective inside the pandemic viewpoints.

At the point when it comes explicitly to advanced education, endeavors to grow the function of nursing in reacting to worldwide malady flare-ups have been put (Corless et al., 2018). Objective identified with readiness has likewise been begun in other advanced education fields (for example see Uhernik, 1998 in advisor instruction; Kaslow, 2004 in proficient brain science; Ng, 2012 in social work). These endeavors ought to be reinforced for a bigger scope and to more fields, for example, educator instruction, agrarian augmentation, transportation examines, united wellbeing, and different fields identified with social administrations in the new typical period.

The COVID-19 pandemic irrefutably found instruction frameworks and students napping. This circumstance uncovered holes in the educational program. One of the means to deliver this hole is to build up a lot of readiness skills framing an objective of the educational plan.

Among Integration and Reduction of Content

With the limitations brought by COVID-19, another typical educational program may likewise receive the reconciliation of substance. This methodology makes it conceivable to lessen the quantity of hours spent on all the subjects yet at the same time tending to all the educational program desires. This technique will empower the digestion of educational program content desires from different subjects in planning a guidance (Romano et al., 2012). For instance, in showing writing, science, and history, substance might be coordinated by experiencing recorded periods and spotlight on logical developments and scholarly works during every period.

Fogarty and Stoehr (1991) proposed a scope of mix models. They presented ten coordination models, for example, divided, associated, and settled, sequenced, shared, webbed, strung, incorporated, submerged, and organised. These models require the osmosis of aptitudes and ideas from different subjects or trains inside an educational program. It could be a decent procedure for instructors to lessen educational plan weights to cover all substance in the midst of the proceeding with limitations.

Besides coordinating the substance, some instructive frameworks are likewise mulling over to decrease the educational plan content. They need to instruct content that is "basic" and eliminate content that isn't. In any case, one significant issue in this proposition lies in the inquiry: How would we characterise "basic" content? Print (1993) exhorted that in choosing content, one must watch a few contemplations. Inside the flow worldwide COVID-19 flare-up, the accompanying three contemplations are recommended by the scientist:

1. *Centrality*: The rule of essentialness applies where substance is considered as far as the fact that it is so principle to the topic under examination. Where the substance is examined as important to the subject, it is considered huge, in this manner suggested for consideration in an educational program.

2. *Significance*: This rule is moored on the truth that substance ought to be identified with the points of view of the network esteems, goals, standards, and issues that would assist students with turning out to be viable residents.

3. *Utility*: Curricularists ought to think about two convenience of the substance: current and future. There is some substance that students need to figure out how to apply in the quick present and other substance to set them up to manage what's to come.

The coming new typical post COVID-19 period can be a workable second for content that is huge, important, and helpful. For example, Gonser (2020) explicitly recommended basic substance, for example, "why cleanliness matters" and "how germs spread" to more unpredictable ones like "moral choices, the science behind how popular contaminations work, or the arithmetic supporting pandemics." Flannery (2020) talked with instructors who incorporated significant substance. One instructor started work with her understudies a subject on Covid antibodies in animals which is a pertinent point both in the overall circumstance and farming social orders. Another instructor seroed in on encouraging another typical conduct called social removing. These are instances of substance that are pertinent in the new ordinary post COVID-19 period.

The COVID-19 condition itself is for sure revamping the substance of the educational plan. Among coordination and decrease of substance, instructors ought to deliberately gauge every alternative without yielding a great part of the information that merits educating to the students.

A Range of Teaching Approaches

Besides numerous instructive frameworks are pondering responsive ways to deal with actualise the educational plan. A large portion of them are investigating the part of innovation. During a period of social removing work on showing a significant new ordinary conduct, numerous schools are going towards complete online methodology or mixed learning methodology in guidance.

The total online methodology of the instructional methodology during the post-COVID-19 time can be possible. For instance, in China that was the principal focal point of the infection, in excess of 180 million youngsters were requested to stay at home. Be that as it may, while schools were shut for isolate, instruction needed to proceed yet this time in a modified methodology. It was executed online through an assortment of online courses and electronic reading material (Patrinos and Shmis, 2020).

Besides, mixed learning is fortuitously known as the "new typical" (Norberg et al., 2011) in the domain of instructive innovation. In spite of the fact that there are obscurities in its definition, mixed learning can be normally depicted as an instructional methodology that incorporates customary homeroom techniques and online advanced strategies (Graham 2013). It requires the physical presence of both instructor and student, with highlights of student authority after some time, setting, or movement (Huang et al., 2009). Given these highlights of mixed learning, it gives favorable possibilities to use in training come new typical occasions.

While complete on the web and mixed learning seems like the "sacred goal" in this new time in instruction, it requires enormous changes. For some created nations, mixed learning is a set up instructive methodology. It has empowered these nations to adapt to the effects of the current COVID-19 plague. Web based learning and instructing are upheld by evolved structures and prepared instructors (Olivier, 2020). Notwithstanding, for different nations, schools should cautiously design virtual learning arrangements. It requires an appraisal of their capacities dependent on the unwavering quality of nearby force supplies, web availability, and status of the instructors (Obana, 2020).

Mixed learning actually requires a measure of customary homeroom methodology. Considering the social separating practice in this new period, bunch work moves toward that require connections with close physical contacts, for example, formal and casual agreeable learning gatherings, think-pair-share, peer guidance, and jigsaw, (Brame and Biel, 2015) may very well be adjusted or diminished, if not disposed of, from the alternatives of instructional strategies for educating.

Then again, there can be more utilisation of techniques that require less development and physical contact. One strategy is immediate guidance. It is an instructional methodology that is arranged, sequenced, and oversaw by the educators. The execution of guidance to students is accomplished fundamentally through procedures like talks or shows. With this technique, educators by and large direct the cycle (The Glossary of Educational Reform, 2013), hence keeping understudies less dynamic.

The COVID-19 worldwide flare-up is clearly reclassifying the ways to deal with instructional execution. The scope of choices that instruction frameworks are examining presents open doors as well as difficulties that must be considered simultaneously.

Updates on Instructional Evaluation

The conclusion of numerous instructive frameworks harmonised with the understudy assessment period in schools. Subsequently, we have seen distinctive instructional assessment rehearses that have been received as a reaction to the COVID-19 emergency. These practices are probably going to be essential for the new typical in instruction. Numerous schools have given actualising rules changing numerous parts of the assessment segment of the educational plan. This time is surely another period in the educational program.

There is enormous replication of instructional assessment to on the web. Inside the online instructional assessment, there are simultaneous and no concurrent structures. The simultaneous structure requires the instructor and the understudy to cooperate at a masterminded time through online applications like Soom. It can likewise be accomplished, for instance, through telephone in which the educator gives appraisal to the students continuously. The no concurrent structure, then again, is the structure wherein the instructor and students don't have to interface online in a live way. They are isolated into various spaces and times. An instrument that is utilised to achieve this evaluation structure is Moodle in which instructor posts appraisal assignments for students (Liberman et al., 2020).

With regards to the evaluating framework, it has been additionally seen that numerous schools have chosen to change their appraisal scales from quantitative to subjective, for example, pass or bomb framework (Farrington, 2020). While the choice is upheld by commendable aims, a few people stress over its belongings. The focal points and hindrances of various appraisal scales are bantered with regards to understudy inspiration (Barnes and Buring, 2012). Inside the contention preferring quantitative over subjective, Dilanchyan (2020) evaluated that such change would segregate the inspiration that understudies need to make progress toward high evaluations.

While the typical quantitative evaluation practice is relied upon to be as yet the predominant practice in the new ordinary, in any case, with the proceeding with worldwide emergency, there will probably be an affinity towards types of mistake in the school appraisal frameworks. Thinking about the troublesome condition of the students, the appraisal develop called tolerance blunder is where the instructor will in general be excessively "liberal" and all understudies are given high passing scores (Nitko and Brookhart, 2014). It is considered as one of the dangers to the dependability of understudy execution which some training partners communicated stresses over.

The COVID-19 emergency is ceaselessly reshaping instructional assessment. The enormous movement of student evaluation to on the web and the changes in accordance with reviewing frameworks are inescapable. With these changes, instructors are urged to keep up great appraisal.

Conclusion

The remarkable effects of the COVID-19 worldwide flare-up are surely guiding instructive frameworks to another ordinary period in mankind's history. This paper endeavoured to re-evaluate training in the new ordinary post COVID-19 period from the point of view of educational plan examines.

An educational plan objective that must be underlined in the new typical educational program is to create readiness abilities among the students. With regards to educational program content, there are difficulties to whether to coordinate or diminish. Then again, instructional methodologies generally moving to online methodology ought to be considered in the light of various elements. As respects instructional assessment, a few concerns identified with the evaluation of learning present relevant updates for teachers.

This paper offers an understanding into how educational program can be reshaped, considering the new typical post COVID-19 period. Different investigates should investigate different parts of training from a more extensive viewpoint. The COVID-19 pandemic influences political, financial, social, and mental measurements. These measurements constantly handled in the rising examinations ought to be additionally inspected to more readily get ready training frameworks in the new period in mankind's history.

References

Mulenga, E. M., & Marbán, J. M. (2020). "Is COVID-19 the gateway for digital learning in mathematics education?" *Contemporary Educational Technology, 12*(2), ep269. https://doi.org/10.30935/cedtech/7949

Naciri, A., Baba, M. A., Achbani, A., & Kharbach, A. (2020). "Mobile learning in higher education: Unavoidable alternative during COVID-19." *Aquademia,* 4(1), ep20016. https://doi.org/10.29333/ aquademia /8227

Nelson, C., Lurie, N., Wasserman, J., & Sakowski, S. (2007). "Conceptualising and defining public health emergency preparedness." *American Journal of Public Health, 97*(1), 9-1. https://doi.org/ 10.2105/AJPH.2007.114496

New normal [Def.1]. (2009). In *Urban Dictionary*. Retrieved on May 1, 2020, from https://www.easybib.com/reference/ guide/apa/ dictionary

Ng, G. (2012) "Disaster work in China: Tasks and competences for social workers." *Social Work Education, 31*(5), 538-556. https://doi.org/ 10.1080/02615479.2011.581277

Nitko, A. J., & Brookhart, S. M. (2014). *Educational assessment of students* (8th ed.). Pearson Education: New York.

Norberg, A., Dsiuban, C. D., & Moskal, P. D. (2011). "A time-based blended learning model." *On the Horison, 19*(3), 207-216. https:// doi.org/10.1108/10748121111163913

Obana, J. (2020, March 18). "Could educational technology be a 'holy grail' amid Covid-19 crisis?" *The Manila Times.* Retrieved from https://www.manilatimes.net/2020/03/18/ business/columnists-business/could-educational-technology-be-a-holy-grail-amid-covid-19-crisis/704202/

Olivier, W. (2020). "Education post-COVID-19: Customised blended learning is urgently needed." *The Conversation.* Retrieved from https://theconversation.com/education-post-covid-19-customised-blended-learning-is-urgently-needed-138647

Patrinos, H. A., & Shmis, T. (2020). "Can technology help mitigate the impact of COVID-19 on education systems in Europe and Central Asia? [Blog post]." Retrieved from https:// blogs. worldbank. org/europeandcentralasia/can-technology-help-mitigate-impact-covid-19-education-systems-europe-and

Print, M. (1993). *Curriculum development and design.* Sydney: SRM Production Services.

Radwan, A., & Radwan, E. (2020). "Social and economic impact of school closure during the outbreak of the COVID-19 pandemic: A quick online survey in the Gasa Strip." *Pedagogical Research, 5*(4), em0068. https://doi.org/ 10.29333/pr/8254

Romano, L., Papa, L., & Saulle, E. (2012). "Awesome lesson ideas to integrate science across the curriculum." *Teach Hub.* Retrieved from http://www.teachhub.com/integrate-science-across-curriculum

3

Education in the COVID-19 Era – Challenges and Opportunities

Aniruddha Burmon

Introduction

The world has been hit with a deadly virus known as Novel (New) Corona Virus which is also known as Corona Virus Disease 2019 (COVID-19). It is pneumonia like respiratory disease. The world has been hit with similar diseases earlier, which also had huge toll on the population. Some of them are Severe Acute Respiratory Syndrome (SARS) in the year 2002 and Middle-East Respiratory Syndrome (MERS) in the year 2012. These are also known as Corona Viruses. Over one million people have already dies because of this COVID-19 pandemic.

It has taken a massive hit on all the sectors of the economy. While it has been slightly easier for Multi-National Companies and professionals to adopt work from home as the new normal and continue business as usual, the times have been challenging for the education system around the world. With disruptions everywhere, several concerned scholars, citisens, politicians, and bureaucrats support the need for reimagining reinventing or rather rebooting the education system. Hence, comes in the smart classroom systems.

The adoption of smart classroom systems by schools is transforming the traditional education system. The sudden switch is not only limited to private schools but even a number of government schools have started running smart classes. Though smart class rooms are not new to educational system but the way it is changing the education fast is unprecedented.

The COVID-19 pandemic has affected educational systems worldwide, leading to the near-total closures of educational institutions everywhere. It has an impact on the continuity of learning for around 300 million young learners in India

It is needless to say, the pandemic has transformed the centuries-old, chalk-talk teaching model to one driven by technology. This disruption in the delivery of education is pushing policymakers to figure out how to drive engagement at scale while ensuring inclusive e-learning solutions and tackling the digital divide.

Merits and Demerits of the Pandemic

Though the crisis is devastating, it is making our schools and even colleges, technologically advanced. No doubt, students and teachers have had to make bigger adjustments as learning has always been in classrooms. Moreover, many of them are not well equipped with technology tools to avail of remote learning.

A multi-pronged strategy is necessary to manage the crisis and build a resilient Indian education system in the long term.

In the first place, immediate measures are essential to ensure continuity of learning in schools and universities. Open-source digital learning solutions and Learning Management Software should be adopted so teachers can conduct teaching online. The DIKSHA platform, of which I will be discussing later in the paper has a reach across all states in India. It can be further strengthened to ensure accessibility of learning to the students.

Secondly, inclusive learning solutions, especially for the most vulnerable and marginalised, need to be developed. Rapid increase of mobile internet users in India is enabling access and personalisation of education even in the remotest parts of the country. This can change the schooling system and increase the effectiveness of learning and teaching, giving students and teachers multiple options to choose from. Many aspirational districts have initiated innovative, mobile – based learning models for effective delivery of education, which can be adopted by others.

Thirdly, strategies are required to prepare the higher education sector for the evolving demand-supply trends across the globe – particularly those related to the global mobility of students and faculty and improving the quality of and demand for higher studies in India. Further, immediate measures are required to mitigate the effects of the pandemic on job offers, internship programs, and research projects.

Fourthly, it is also important to reconsider the current methods of teaching in schools and higher education institutions by integrating classroom learning with e-learning modes to build a unified learning system. The major challenge in Educational Technology reforms at the national level is the seamless integration of technology in the present Indian education system, which is the most diverse and largest in the world. Further, it is also important to establish quality assurance mechanisms and quality benchmark for online learning developed and offered by India Higher Educational Institutions (HEIs) as well as e-learning platforms (growing rapidly). Many e-learning players offer multiple courses on the same subjects with different levels of certifications, methodology and assessment parameters. So, the quality of courses may differ across different e-learning platforms.

Lastly, the Indian traditional knowledge may also be integrated with a present-day mainstream university education to serve the larger cause of humanity.

In this time of crisis, a well-rounded and effective educational practice is what is needed for the capacity-building of young minds. It will develop skills that will drive their employability, productivity, health, and well-being in the decades to come, and ensure the overall progress of India.

Shift of Focus

- We have already observed that there is a shift of focus from teaching to learning
- The delivery system is no longer teacher centric. It is learner centric.
- Education is no longer defined in terms of what a teacher will teach but rather in terms of what a student will be able to demonstrate.
- "To learn is to change. Education is a process that changes the learner." – George Leonard
- We have moved from an instruction paradigm, in which an instructor transfers knowledge to students, to a learning paradigm, in which a teacher's role is that of a coach. The result is a student learning how to learn and discovering knowledge with the coaching guidance of a teacher.
- There are Group Activities and Brain Storming sessions

COVID-19 Challenge

With the coming of COVID-19 we have become used to the phrase Social Distancing which actually means Physical Distancing.

We have become used to online classes and even online examinations.

Resources to Provide Psycho – Social Support

People cannot go out of houses and everything has changed around them. Children mostly cannot go out and play. They are feeling depressed. Hence, the UNESCO has provided for psychosocial support for people during the pandemic. An Inter-Agency Standing Committee guideline to protect and improve people's mental health and psychosocial well-being in the midst of an emergency has been initiated.

The World Health Organisation (WHO) has initiated mental health and psychosocial guidance during the COVID-19 outbreak.

The United Nations International Childrens' Educational Fund (UNICEF) has talked of guidance on how teachers should talk to children about COVID-19 and on how parents and care givers can talk to children about COVID-19

Resources Available

Below mentioned are some resources available. Some of which are available in the UNESCO website. Some of these resources are:

Digital Learning Management Systems

There are quite a few Digital Learning Management Systems. Some of these are Century Tech, Class Dojo, Edmodo, Edraak, EkStep, Google Classroom, Moodle, Nafham etc.

Systems Built for use on Basic Mobile Phones

Systems built for use on basic mobile phones are Cell-Ed, Enesa Education, Funsi, KaiOS, Ubongo, Ustad Mobile, Kolibri, Rumie,

Other resources available are Radio, TV, YouTube live, Facebook live, Swayamprabha etc. Swayamprabha is a group of 32 DTH channels aimed at secondary, higher secondary, UG & PG levels. Presently 12 channels are promoting learning for classes 1 – 12.

Massive Open Online Course (MOOC) platforms

Some of the Massive Open Online Course (MOOC) Platforms are Alison, Canvas Network, Coursera, European Schoolnet Academy, EdX, i Course, Future Learn, Icourses, TED-Ed Earth School, XuetangX, Udemy, Unacademy, SWAYAM, openculture.com, UK Open University etc.

National Repository of Open Educational Resources (NROER)

National Repository of Open Educational Resources (NROER) was started in 2013 by the Ministry of Human Resource Development

(MHRD). It was developed by National Council of Educational Research and Training (NCERT). It contains open resources for classes one to twelve. Audio, video document and interactive contents are available here.

National Initiative for School Heads and Teachers Holistic Advancement (NESTA)

This is an effective programme to train heads of schools, resource persons and teachers at the elementary school level. This is a capacity building programme.

TESS INDIA – Teacher Education for School based Support

Here one can get audio, video or written materials for classes I to VIII. The contents are available in different Indian languages.

Mobile Reading Applications

Some mobile reading applications are African Storybook, Biblioteca Digital del Institute Latinoamericano de la Comunicación Educativa, Global Digital Library, Interactive Learning Program, Reads, Room to Read, StoryWeaver, Worldreader, Kindle, E-book etc.

Collaboration Platforms that support Live – Video Communication

Some collaboration platforms that support live-video communication are Dingtalk, Lark, Hangouts Meet, MS Teams, Skype, WeChat Work, WhatsApp etc.

Some additional Platforms are Cisco Webex, Google Meet, Google Classroom, Team Link, TCS Glassroom, Coursera, GoToMeet, Canvas etc.

Tools for Teachers to create Digital Learning Content are as follows:

- Thinglink – Tools to create interactive images, videos and other multimedia resources.

- Buncee – Supports the creation and sharing visual representations of learning content, including media-rich lessons, reports, newsletters and presentations.
- EdPussle – Video lesson creation software.
- EduCaixa – Courses in Spanish language to help teachers develop the skills and competencies of learners in areas such as communication, entrepreneurship, STEM and big data.
- Kaltura – Video management and creation tools with integration options for various learning management systems.
- Nearpod – Software to create lessons with informative and interactive assessment activities.
- Pear Deck – Facilitates the design of engaging instructional content with various integration features.
- Squigl – Content creation platform that transforms speech or text into animated videos.
- Trello – A visual collaboration tool used by teachers and professors for easier coursework planning, faculty collaboration, and classroom organisation.

External Repositories of Distance Learning Solutions are as follows:

- Brookings – A catalogue of nearly 3,000 learning innovations. Not all of them are distance learning solutions, but many of them offer digital education content.
- Common Sense Education – Tips and tools to support school closures and transitions to online and at-home learning.
- Commonwealth of Learning – List of resources for policymakers, school and college administrators, teachers,

parents and learners that will assist with student learning during the closure of educational institutions.

- Education Nation – Nordic countries have opened up their learning solutions for the world for free, supporting teachers and learners during the school closures.
- EdSurge – Community-driven list of edtech products, including many distance learning resources for students, teachers and schools, covering primary to post-secondary education levels.
- European Commission Resources – A collection of online platforms for teachers and educators, available in 23 EU languages.

There are more External Repositories which are e-pathshala, e-pgpathshala, National Digital Library of India, West Bengal Secretariat Library, West Bengal Public Library Network, e-shodhganga, e-shodhsuddhi, tagoreweb, Gandhi Sevagram Ashram, Romeo Sherpa, Spoken Tutorial, Free and Open Source Software for Education (FOSSEE), e-Yantra, National Knowledge Network (NKN), National Project on Technology Enhanced Learning (NPTEL), NMEICT, National Academic Depository (NAD), SHAGUN, Diksha, National Repository of Open Educational Resource (NROER) etc.

All these enhance our ability to connect easily with institutions and enhance our access to learning resources. For instance, National Knowledge Network (NKN) provides high speed network backbone to educational institutes in India. The online assessment agencies/private business houses are also improving the product, considering the limited bandwidth and physical distancing, by managing remotely proctored examinations/skilling assessments. Basic requirements like sturdy education delivery platforms, IT infrastructure, PC/Desktop/Mobile for end-delivery and assessment tools have been planned and more improvement is underway.

For countries like India, this is a good opportunity to strengthen the internet connectivity across rural India. Every village and town in India should be digitally connected for better interaction between the students and teachers. Institutes like IITs have "a sort" of infrastructure to connect students but the experience shows that not all students have good interaction due to various reasons.

According to Dr Francisco Marmolejo, advisor to Qatar Foundation in India, during his webinar, held by the Jio International Institute, India, higher education should be re-designed. It should be flexible, more innovative, more international but more locally connected and socially responsible, more collaborative and less risk-averse. Innovative models should be introduced. Universities/institutes could be online-providing internet-based flexible offerings (open universities); traditional learning with hand-on work; collaboration with other schools.

We have been talking about virtual classrooms and various online tools today allow us to make the engagement between the teacher and students as close to a real, in classroom type experience, as possible. Going forward, these tools can also make the teachers and parent meetings as well as staff/management meetings more time and cost saving while providing the necessary interactivity.

It is up to the Govt. to take initiatives to provide free internet services to the remotest corners of the country and provide handsets to every child.

I can recall the OLPC project that started in Africa at the rate of $100 per laptop announced by One Laptop Per Child (OLPC) non-profit organisation founded by MIT professor Nicholas Negroponte in 2005. The OLPC project was a classic example of a device designed to help the Third World. It had very limited success. In India people thought we could make laptops at a much lower cost which actually proved otherwise.

One may recall the BBC Micros that were bought by the Indian government in the late 1980s was a failure too.

Presently Mid-day Meal Project is basically stopped. This money can easily be used to improve internet connectivity and give learners access to mobile handsets.

Pedagogy in digital education is an important link between course content, educationists, technology and course-takers. Democratisation of technology is now an important issue, comprising internet connectivity, telecom infrastructure, affordability of online system, availability of laptop/desktop, software, educational tools, online assessment tools, etc. But it is a fact that technology-based education is more transparent and does not make difference in front vs. back benchers or girls vs. boys.

COVID-19 has prompted experts to rethink the conventional mode of education. Digital education appears to be a viable solution to fill in the void for classroom education. A complete revolution in the way we learn today has been brought about by Technology. Each student gets in contact with a world-class education, which is not easy to impart by the traditional white chalk and blackboard method of teaching. A multi-pronged strategy is necessary to manage the crisis and build a resilient Indian education system in the long term. This is an ideal time to accept technology and its latest offerings in order to make education delivery to students more efficient and make it more productive through online learning and assessments," said Kiran Dham, CEO of Globus Infocom Ltd.

It is a fact that the government of India as well state governments, through their various ministries/departments, have created infrastructure to deliver e-education.

"The impact of COVID-19 will remain for years, if not longer. The new normal will be that significantly larger numbers of students will attend classes from home. While this trend was already on the uptick, it will receive a massive impetus because of COVID-19. The great thing is that India is well prepared to teach lakhs of students at home. The country has one of the world's most extensive 4G networks on the planet. In virtually every part of the country, there is 4G connectivity. Even more impressive is the fact that data is very affordable. Over such robust networks, classes can be streamed with ease. Students who learn in virtual classrooms will find that their learning experience is as good as or maybe even better than that of students who sit in classes. The hugely transformative power of virtual classrooms is their ability to bring an endless number of courses to students' doorsteps. A student living in the interior of the country can master a course on AI or big data without paying a considerable fee. Indeed, over the next few years, the number of students who get an education online will grow considerably," said IntelliPaat Founder and CEO Diwakar Chittora.

Conclusion

Going forward, the use of technology in teaching or recruitment will lead to a new era wherein the best of faculty will be available from across the globe to students. Education quality will be gauged not just by the quality of faculty but will also have quality of IT infrastructure and familiarisation of the faculty with digital teaching technologies as important parameters. The physical infrastructure of academic institutions will have less impact on the quality of education and thus directly on the cost of education. Review meetings, parent-teacher meetings, subject conferences will be location agnostic. The real vision of the new education policy for liberal education will get executed. It is possible that in times to come, a student may be allowed to carry out courses from any College/University based on quality of teacher and fees for the course irrespective of his location and finally will get degree from the home university where s/he got registered or from the university where he has taken maximum courses, resulting in a balance of economics of good education. For all this to be a reality, a drastic change in thought process is required in the mind-set of policy makers, authorities, students and specially educationists. Faculty selection should gradually be linked to technology friendliness and keenness for technology adoption. Similarly, accreditation parameters, criteria need reconsideration. All these steps will help strengthen the country's digital learning infrastructure in the long run. Covid-19 has only accelerated adoption of technologies to deliver education.

Apart from these we also need to look at the problems of Persons with Disabilities (PWDs). They need a lot of support and empathy. Digital solutions may be available but many of them may not be in a position to use these gadgets. A lot of funds are necessary to support them. All these years they have been taught to do things in one sort of way, now in most cases they have to unlearn most of these and learn new things which are being extremely hard on them, their teachers, their parents/guardians and even care givers.

References

https://timesofindia.indiatimes.com/blogs/dornadula-c/post-covid-19-education-system/ May 15, 2020, 8:25 PM IST

https://government.economictimes.indiatimes.com/news/education/covid-19-pandemic-impact-and-strategies-for-education-sector-in-india/75173099 April 16, 2020, 09:45 IST

https://www.financialexpress.com/education-2/covid-19-how-smart-classrooms-are-transforming-indias-education-system/1948670/ May 5, 2020 2:02 PM

https://www.indiatoday.in/education-today/featurephilia/story/covid-19-lockdown-how-the-pandemic-brining-change-in-indian-education-system-1674322-2020-05-04 May 4, 2020 18:36 IST

https://www.latestlaws.com/articles/impact-of-covid-19-on-education-system-in-india/ 16 May 2020

https://en.unesco.org/covid19/educationresponse/solutions

https://english.mathrubhumi.com/education/articles/education-in-covid-19-scenario-challenges-and-opportunities-1.4880403

http://jgu.edu.in/blog/2020/06/29/impact-of-covid-19-on-higher-education-challenges-opportunities/ JUNE 29, 2020

https://www.iau-aiu.net/COVID-19-Higher-Education-challenges-and-responses accessed 21-10-2020 8.37 (IST)

https://www.brookings.edu/blog/education-plus-development/2020/04/10/top-10-risks-and-opportunities-for-education-in-the-face-of-covid-19/ Friday, April 10, 2020 https://www.brookings.edu/president/covid-19-a-moment-for-unity/ Saturday, March 21, 2020

https://www.un.org/development/desa/dspd/wpcontent/uploads/sites/22/2020/08/sg_policy_brief_covid-19_and_education_august_2020.pdf

www.globaldev.blog › blog › educational-challenges-c

4

Challenges before Laboratory Based Subjects in India during Covid-19 Pandemic

Bhaskar Chaudhuri

Relevance of Online Learning in Higher Education

The online techniques of imparting higher education have become popular in recent time due to several factors. The Covid-19 Pandemic has made online teaching-learning mandatory all over the world. E-learning has remained a 'recent advance' in technical education due to the ongoing change and advancement in the information technology and introduction of more user-friendly methods of e-learning. Recently online education has been studied widely and has been compared with the usual method of teaching in various papers. Despite some drawbacks that e-learning can be an efficient addition to the conventional method of teaching and learning (Choules, 2007).

Rajendran et al. (2010) mentioned about learning inducing a constant, measurable, and particular behavioural change in the learner to create a new mental construct or modify a prior mental construct. The learning styles may be classified into four methods:

a) Auditory learning, i.e. learning by hearing

b) Visual learning, i.e. learning by seeing only

c) Reading / writing, i.e. learning by processing contents

d) Kinaesthetic learning or practical, i.e. learning by experimenting things.

In the audio-visual stage, education is imparted through Visuals combined with auditory. So, visuals suggest not only pictures but also 3D as well as 2D videos. The mode of teaching through Computers is called Computer Based Training often abbreviated as CBT. Through CBT, a student derives knowledge about how a system will look alike plus how it works. CBT raises the level of education, but again it also has a flip side to it. Now a student can know the modus operandi of a system, but the student may not be able to experiment with the system. Thus the students suffer from cognitive knowledge. Another important learning style is kinaesthetic learning, means learning by doing. It helps the students to build up logical reasoning. Simple experiments can be conducted as a laboratory, but there are few complex experiments which are not possible in labs. In those conditions, virtual labs are useful. Virtual Labs have substantial educational potential as they provide a chance to 'learn by doing' and also provide access to systems which are unreachable due to safety, cost and sise issues. Users can look at a diversity of input and observe the output. Thus, virtual labs have many advantages. The study seeks to recognise the efficiency of these virtual labs in E-learning suite.

Diwakar et al. (2014) found that virtual labs offered a relative advantage to learn neurophysiology and neuron modelling vis-à-vis conventional classroom education. Assignments, simulations and quisses improved student content interactions even as personalising their aptitude to respond as well as interact. Most students learned interacting with virtual laboratory exercises and improved in presenting classroom exercises. Kocijancic and O'Sullivan (2004) viewed that an accepted ICT-enabled tool can be used to simulate a classroom laboratory experience.

Virtual labs allow remote ease of access to appropriate environments and ease blended learning. These tools offer a learning experience analogous to that of a classroom laboratory, especially for those lacking laboratory experience in addition to the distance learning community in general (Kennepohl and Shaw, 2010; Achuthan et al., 2011).

India has developed its own pioneering examples of freely obtainable e-learning resources. Scientific-education materials, for example, those provided by the Sakshat Virtual Labs and the National Programme on Technology Enhanced Learning, are also accessible to the international audience (Ray et al. 2012). The application of mobile has become important because of technology-based education. Mobile learning has become trendy since the smartphones are being used by medical students internationally and therefore form a simple platform to introduce education through it. With the arrival of smartphones, mobile-learning has become easier due to a variety of internet platforms like WhatsApp, Google groups, and Facebook (Jamal, et al., 2016).

The practical subjects are dependent on laboratories for experiments. The natural science subjects do active experiments, whereas social science subjects like geography mostly depend on instruments for measuring heights or quantitative techniques for socio-economic analysis of field surveys. However, the pandemic of 2020 has disturbed the teaching-learning scenario worldwide in general and the developing countries in particular. It is difficult to conduct practical experiments in a situation when there are several restrictions to move outside. The University Grants Commission as well as universities has found it perplexing to implement an effective strategy to conduct practical subjects. As a result, most of these subjects have nowadays become confined to theoretical aspects only. This has resulted in inadequate learning and lack of understanding of these subjects (Sawahel, 2020).

Sharma (2019) found that pathology could be learned as a dynamic discipline for clinical problem-solving. An essential feature of pathology is microscopic slide-based learning. So, it is considered as one of the most difficult exercises by the students. The difficulty the students face is fundamentally owing to failure to remember the visual images of the pathologic findings found under the microscope. This difficulty can be potentially solved by frequent viewing of the microscopic images by the students using slide projections or by different e-learning platforms. Prior introduction of the microscopic slides by application, the WhatsApp could be an effective method of priming the students before the usual microscopy teaching in pathology practical. This facet of pathology practical teaching has been under – researched.

International Experiences

The virtual learning techniques experimented in many countries even before the pandemic. According to Michael (2020), the American Association of Chemistry Teachers or AACT has a good collection of activities, projects, animations, simulations and videos to teach chemistry online.

Alchemie is a game-based chemistry learning tool which students can access on their smartphones. During COVID – 19, Alchemie offers full free access to Mechanisms, considered as the first and only tool for organic chemistry. It enables students to learn as well as practice reaction mechanisms by moving and also manipulating individual bonds and electrons.

Flinn Scientific really offered free resources during the crisis which included:

- Free video labs with teachers and students guides to help students at home continue improving on key science topics.
- Free, simple and fun-to-do activities use normally available resources to promote scientific investigation in the home
- On-call scientists: Flinn normally broadcasts live laboratory experiments conducted by scientific people. Flinn is equipped with a team of scientists who answer questions from teachers and students teaching and studying online.
- Inq-ITS is a science learning technology with simulations for physical science, life science as well as earth science, as per NGSS standards. During the pandemic condition, Inq-ITS offer access to their total collection of virtual science laboratories.

- Pasco offers home science tools free of cost for the remainder of 2020 along with six months free access to Capstone and SPARK vue software. Besides free access to Essential Physics and Essential Chemistry curriculum are also provided.
- Vernier's high-quality interactive videos provide students with the opening to observe plus study 'hard-to-replicate experiments' no matter where they are. Hundreds of interactive problems and free experiments with sample data files are obtainable to teachers by free trial during the pandemic related suspension of classes.

India can adopt Virtual Laboratories

The Indian system of education follows traditional teaching methods. There is little emphasis on innovation, lack of investment in education, and industry-academia interface is conspicuous by its absence. The laboratory-based education in India is expensive to set up and requires the active involvement of government in providing infrastructures. In privately-owned institutions, such education is very costly. The students fund the cost of education in private institutions. It makes receiving an education in science and technology expensive for students. Despite this fact, many privately owned institutions in India have started developing virtual laboratories for imparting quality education.

Experts believe, as mentioned by (Rajendran et al., 2010: 2175) that this technology would survive and flourish in the industry. These virtual labs will aid the students in remote regions. They can learn the concepts by themselves, thus increasing their performance and competence in the area of their specialisation. The system is efficient as it will be commercially viable for the students. They can conduct the experiments at home or schools, or anywhere. The rural areas suffer from lack of facility to provide laboratories for the students can be minimised by applying virtual lab technologies. For example, when teaching networking, it is unattainable to establish a full infrastructure in an institute of higher learning. It is highly expensive to set up laboratories with full equipment. Hence, Virtual labs could be a viable option. NIIT provides facilities of virtual Lab and Simulation software for teaching networking. The students can reap the benefits of using this software as they can experiment with the network architecture without any complexity. Another great benefit of using simulation software and virtual labs is that students can effectively work from home.

The use of virtual laboratories in a developing country such as India is essential not only because of the Covid-19 pandemic of 2020 but also because establishing a physical laboratory and constantly upgrading it is a financially difficult option. It may be probable to apply virtual laboratories in selected subjects or topics for ease of teaching and learning.

Dearnley et al. (2008) and Mayfield et al. (2013) found that with the introduction of smartphones, 'mobile-learning' via internet platforms such as WhatsApp, Google groups, and YouTube have become a trend of E-learning now. Studies suggest that mobile learning supports teaching and learning (Sharma, 2019). WhatsApp is at present one of the most extensively used social networking platform. Consequently, WhatsApp could be a 'readymade' platform to commence E-learning at no additional cost or logistics.

References

Choules, A. P. (2007). "The use of E-learning in medical education: a review of the current situation." *Postgraduate Medical Journal, 83*(978), 212-216.

Dearnley, C., Haigh, J., & Fairhall, J. (2008). "Using mobile technologies for assessment and learning in practice settings: A case study." *Nurse education in practice, 8*(3), 197-204.

Diwakar, S., Parasuram, H., Medini, C., Raman, R., Nedungadi, P., Wiertelak, E., Srivastava, S., Achuthan, K, & Nair, B. (2014). "Complementing neurophysiology education for developing countries via cost-effective virtual labs: case studies and classroom scenarios." *Journal of undergraduate neuroscience education, 12*(2), A130.

Kocijancic, S., & O'Sullivan, C. (2004). "Real or virtual laboratories in science teaching-Is this actually a dilemma?." *Informatics in Education*, *3*(2), 239-250.

Sharma, C. (2019). "Impact of adding E-learning to the conventional pathology practical teaching." *IP Archives of Cytology and Histopathology Research*, 4, 1-10, doi: 10.18231/2456-9267.2019.0001

Mayfield, C. H., Ohara, P. T., & O'Sullivan, P. S. (2013). "Perceptions of a mobile technology on learning strategies in the anatomy laboratory." *Anatomical sciences education*, *6*(2), 81-89.

Michael, Connor (2020). *LSI's Guide to Teaching Science during the COVID-19 Shutdown*, Mar 18, Lab Safety, Retrieved from https://www.labsafety.org/teaching-science-during-covid-19-shutdown

Rajendran, L., Veilumuthu, R. & Divya, J. (2010). "A Stduy on the effectiveness of virtual lab in E-learning." *International Journal on Computer Science and Engineering*, 2(6).

Ray, Sandipan; Nicole R. Koshy, Shyam Diwakar, Bipin Nair, Sanjeeva Srivastava (2012). "Sakshat Labs: India's virtual proteomics initiative." *PLOS Bio*logy *10(7)*. https://doi.org/10.1371/ journal.pbio.1001353.

Sawahel, Wagdy (COVID-19 drives development of online laboratories, 16 July 2020, Retrieved from https://www.university worldnews.com/post.php?story=20200715130543961

5

Digital Discrimination and Primary School Education in the Time of Covid-19: Concerns and Challenges in India

Bidushi Saha

Introduction

The outbreak of SARS-COV-2 Virus, leading to the global pandemic has turned the year, 2020 as one of the most challenging years in the world history. The Covid-19 pandemic has affected almost all the countries of the world. While some countries face stagnation in growth and serious health security issues, almost all face challenges to their education systems. India is amongst those countries whose educational institutions, including schools, have been shut down since March, 2020 in light of the spread of Covid-19. To continue the teaching-learning process, a new alternative has been adopted by almost all educational institutions and as a result, the traditional classrooms have been shifted to the digital platform. It is in this context that an understanding of the impact of Covid-19 on primary school education in India garners importance with special focus on the children who are digitally deprived of online education, leading to digital discrimination and exclusion.

The RTE Act of India ensures free and compulsory elementary education to all children belonging to the age group 6-14. The term "compulsory education" casts an obligation on the appropriate Central or State government, under Section 8 of the RTE Act, to provide and ensure compulsory admission, attendance and completion of elementary education by every child of the age of 6-14 (Despande, 2020, para.7). But Covid-19 has put restrictions on the traditionally practiced classroom-based teaching and learning in primary schools, compelling the schools to adopt the digitally driven mode of teaching-learning assessment. But the scenario is something that is not only vulnerable but a matter of serious concern too. UNESCO Report (2020) indicates that over 60 percent of the world's student population is affected by school closures and that trust in public education services is undermined and could potentially corrode human rights in the present and post pandemic world (Jahangeer, 2020, para.2). In the present decade, India has made a significant progress on schooling and enrolment rates in primary education sector by taking various effective central and state policies. Though dropout rates and low level of learning in primary schools remain challenges for the government, the pandemic has created more challenges in primary education level during the pandemic that need to be addressed with utmost priority.

Universalisation of elementary education has given the highest priority since the Independence of India. Properly planned educational input contributes to the national growth and development, to cultural richness, to effective and efficient governance. Indian economy has an inevitable relation to rural economy and universalisation of elementary education has an important role to play here. Education Statistics At A Glance (2018), published by The Department of School Education & Literacy, Government of India states that India has achieved a literacy rate of 64% in 2018-2019; but the gross number of illiterates is the highest in the world (para.6). So, it can be easily estimated that the access to elementary education is going to play an important role in Post-Pandemic Indian economy.

The Department of School Education & Literacy, Government of India, estimates that there are 840546 government primary schools in India. The Covid-19 pandemic has created an alternative but essential need for technological infrastructure. But in a developing country like India, the matter of online education in primary schools during the Covid-19 pandemic has clearly widened the persistent socio-economic inequality of Indian society. The 2019 global multi-dimensional poverty index report by the United Nations states that 22% of Indian population live below the poverty line ("Corona Virus," 2020, p.A6). According to the Broadcast India Survey (2018), only 23.8% households across India had internet facilities with 1.3 billion people having smart phones. The Niti Aayog in its Strategy for New India@75 Report, highlighted the quality and reliability of the internet as a major bottleneck. It also pointed out that 55000 villages in India are without mobile network coverage (Pandey, 2020, para.7). Banerjee et al. (2015) in *Power for All: Electricity Access Challenge In India* reported that about 311 million people still live without electricity, about 93% reside in rural areas and 40% are in the poorest income group. Bihar has the lowest overall access rate, at 25%, followed by Uttar Pradesh at 43%, Orissa at 56%, West Bengal at 59%, and Rajasthan at 77%. By contrast, 13 states have successfully provided electricity to more than 90% of their poorest population (p.2). Therefore, the learners belonging to the population without electricity and electronic devices are unable to be included in the digitally driven teaching – learning process during the pandemic period.

However, this alternative digitally driven e-learning reveals stark persistent reality of inequality of Indian society in terms of availability of resources and access to these online classes. These digital initiatives are also perpetuating the hegemony of elite schools over the education system, resulting in the digital divide between rural and urban, between rich and poor. It should be noted that all the narratives of digitally driven online education during the pandemic in the primary schools of India is the question of equity and equality. The expectation that learners of elementary level will access technology to receive education at their own cost and the failure to provide requisite infrastructure by governments, including learning equipment – both fall foul of the RTE Act. So, a large section of learners are left out of the online education system, being a subject to digital discrimination and exclusion.

Conclusion

The current situation is, of course, an unpredicted one. The matter of digital discrimination and exclusion in terms of online education in primary schools in India during the pandemic is not only associated with the poor but also with the linguistic minorities, gender minorities and learners with disabilities. The elementary education in government schools in India, especially for learners from rural areas and the urban poor background, is witnessing unprecedented challenges caused by Covid-19 pandemic and thereby questions the objectives of RTE Act 2009.

References

Banerjee, Sudeshna, Barnes, Douglas, Singh, Bipul, Mayer, Kristy, & Samad, Hussain (2015) *Power for All: Electricity Access Challenge In India.* Washington DC: The World Bank.

Corona Virus. (2020, June 13), *The Hindu*, p.A6.

Despande, Rohan (2020, June 8). "Digital Education and Covid19: Addressing the tragic state Of Students in the Indian Education System." *The Leaflet.* Retrieved from http://www. theleaflet.in

Department of School Education & Literacy, Government of India. (2018). *Education Statistics At A Glance 2018.*Retrieved from http://www. stats.gov.in

Jahangeer, Khalid (2020, August 2). "Let's Shift Our Focus to 'Education Pandemic' in India." *The Eastern Herald.* Retrieved from http://www. easternherald.com

Pandey, Vidhu (2020, June 24). "India's Education System Feels Digital Divide Amid the Pandemic." *The Diplomat.* Retrieved from http://www. thediplomat.com

6

Online Education in India during Covid-19 Pandemic: Challenges and Opportunities

Bitasta Goswami

Introduction

Education is the backbone of every nation state, without which their economic success would remain as a distant dream. A developed nation is inexorably an educated nation. India as a developing nation is continuously evolving in the education field since its Independence. Recent release of the NEP Draft in the year 2019 has been welcomed, with its fair share of dismay and protest, with a siseable section of its stake holders harbouring suspicion over its intent and content. Since 1967 practices and concepts of educational planning have undergone substantial changes. Although there have been lot of encumbrance to education system of India but nevertheless there have been a lot of opportunities to cope with these challenges for betterment of the system. Undoubtedly, the biggest challenge faced by the education system of India since Independence is the lockdown situation created due to COVID-19 pandemic crisis in the year 2020. Schools and colleges across India were shut down since mid-March in the year 2020 as the government recuperated to control the spread of coronavirus. For most schools, colleges and universities this hindered the examination schedule, creating much uncertainty about the impact of the lockdown on the academic calendar. Lockdown situation compelled the Indian education system to shift from age old chalk and duster system to online education, e-teaching and e-learning became the only solution of this crisis situation as students and teachers were locked down in their respective houses and virtual medium was the only hope in the era of social distancing which was strictly followed by the government norms. Telelectures were conducted through national news channels, online classes were provided through various online platforms like Google meet, Soom etc.

Challenges

There are certain disadvantages of online education in India. For instance, the public schools and universities are not that much well equipped like private schools and universities. Entire student community do not have digital facilities, some students come from far remote places where technology is not available. In India, there is a central system of education, different states have different languages; if study materials are distributed digitally in English or Hindi most students are unable to grasp it because of their vernacular training bases. To sum up the challenges of Digital teaching and learning – first problem is teachers lack knowledge on e-teaching and e-learning pedagogy, and this problem exist in both the generations of experienced teachers as well as young teachers. Secondly, deprived areas are lacking technological support, there is no availability of TV connection so the question remains how they are going to attend the tele lectures, moreover with unavailability of high-speed internet network, unstable electricity connection, unavailability of gadgets, affordability of equipment and inadequate e-learning infrastructure; e-learning remains a distant dream to most of the student community. This is creating a digital divide among students. However, COVID-19 has exposed the e-learning challenges of India and provides an excellent opportunity for the country to speed up the building of tech and digital start-ups as well as to significantly increase the access of affordable and reliable high-speed internet facility in under – served areas. Hence digital education has a good chance of significant growth during this crisis situation.

Opportunities

According to some academician it is said that, for the schools and universities in India the lockdown has come as a "blessing in disguise", and the fright of poor quality of online teaching and teacher's hesitation to use online portals have now completely disappeared. Online teaching and learning have become a reality in today's world of global pandemic crisis and should be fully incorporated into the educational system. It is evident that younger population are at advantageous position in this eLearning process while the older generation is adopting with it in a slower manner as they are less tech savvy. Digital teaching's advantages include it can reach to wider audiences from faraway places, e-teaching is a commodity for which we shall all strive for and we must plan in a democratic manner keeping in mind that no discrimination is carried on the weak, vulnerable and less privileged communities, robust and good internet facility must be provided to all in an affordable range. Democratic and inclusive character of e-teaching demolishes borders and provides a wider platform to different places in the world, and gives teachers and professors the independence to transfer their knowledge freely to create more responsible open-minded students. There are multiple advantages of eLearning in the situation of emergency but feedback came from students that though they are adopting with eLearning process, they do not enjoy this process and will prefer classroom learning as situation gets normalised. Hence eLearning can only be the reliable temporary substitute at the time of national crisis only when physical participation in the normal classroom scenario is not possible.

Recommendations

In the education sector, our immediate priority during the lockdown and thereafter must be to focus and built up our knowledge on Information Technology infrastructure for Covid like situations in future. The online teaching methodology should focus on coalesced e-learning and quality of its e-resources. UGC and erstwhile MHRD or as we call today Ministry of Education, must look after the quality of internet, affordability of high-speed connectivity and security of e-portals as major issues for the immediate attention of the government. All Universities must take into consideration that hundred percent students' strength can access these e-learning facilities. Every schools and colleges in rural and urban India must introduce a compulsory computer course to make their students proficient in e-learning process. Indian universities need to focus on effective mode of online classroom, workshops and seminars, or as we are calling it webinars! It is also important that both teachers and students create the task of building a more professionally oriented teaching-learning environment during the conduct of online classes and other online activities. Education system of each and every State must make sure that the maximum utilisation of online systems is enabled to prepare the students not only for the immediate goal of completing the coursework for the current academic year but also to plan beyond and groom them for tomorrow's knowledge-intensive and technology-driven educational environment. Inclusive learning process should be there and vulnerable and marginalised societies must not be overlooked, technology must be available to all societies of students. A unified well rounded and effective practical educational strategy should be created by the central government to facilitate entire student's community to take care of their educational as well as mental and physical health.

Global Scenario

Globally, the pandemic situation is dictating that the inevitable e-l earning process as the only option of this current crisis. Initially Indian think-tank was not digitally geared up for the lockdown and though Indian statistics were still comparatively lower than the global statistics of death rate and number of contamination and hospitalisation of corona positive patients but now it is also clear that this is only the first cycle of infection, and gradually the numbers are increasing at a steeper rate, second cycle will be coming and we have to be prepared for the future scenario, just like Spanish influensa. Technology is the only solution in this "Black swan" situation which will overcome the future volatility, uncertainty and ambiguity. US-China antagonism is building up due to this Covid-19 pandemic which is an unhealthy way of dealing things and it is affecting the global scenario, both should behave more maturely and as world leaders must resolve their antagonism for a better world's future. Secondly, the world might be enhancing towards a great economic depression like 1930s, as WTO data states that we are marching towards a vicious cycle of economic recession which will result into rise in number of unemployment and low GDP growth rate. International organisations like the 'white elephant' UN, 'politicised' WTO and 'confused' WHO are at loggerheads whereas they should have tried collaborative efforts to cope with the menace. At the age of globalisation, as we call ourselves global citisens living in a global village this pandemic will increase the gap between developed nations with their 'fortress kind of mentality' and developing nations creating a further interstate and intra state migration problem and economic stresses which in the turn will rip the socio-economic structure cooperative culture of the world. Governments will be more effective if they choose to be quasi authoritarian regime to deal with the situation, security measures will be of immense importance, soft power or smart power will be more important than hard power, defense budget is going to decrease giving an impetus to health sector rejuvenation. Technology will build a new class distinction in the digital society of have's and have-not's, national as well as international organisations must look into these issues in a post Covid world with digital practices moving towards e-governance, e-health, e-learning creating a better technology driven world.

Conclusion

Self-motivating students will succeed in this online-learning scenario but it is needed that different strategies, methods and styles must be adopted to reach greater number of students including flexibility and accessibility of quality learning. Current situation might increase students thinking skills and social skills as well working towards empathy where teachers have lost direct control and supervision on students. Though this social distancing during the pandemic is been called the "new normal" situation but in disagreement with this notion, it is rather an abnormal situation. Soon the global pandemic will be in control and the crisis time will pass, in the meantime students should focus on the positive sides and grasp the opportunities of online education and hopefully in near future we will revert back to our normal classroom scenario. Undoubtedly, Covid-19 pandemic is creating a challenge in the learning process but it is also giving us an opportunity to reform the education system for better future learning potentials in India. In a Covid free world, working from home while e-teaching and e-learning mode may become the alarming reality of the day. This would also impose a radical change in the way we offer education in our schools and universities and concoct them for the rapidly changing e-knowledge environment of the education sector. The experience gained during the pandemic crisis should pave the way for India's future reforms in the education sector and hopefully it will be incorporated in NEP to prepare us for tomorrow's post Covid world.

References

DD news. UGC forms committee to encourage online learning amid lockdown. Retrieved on April 16, 2020 from http://ddnews.gov.in/national/ugc-forms-committee-encourage-online-learning-amid-lockdown

https://government.economictimes.indiatimes.com/ news/education /how-lockdown-reveals-actual-state-of-e-education-in-india/75803841

https://www.financialexpress.com/education-2/online-learning-and-education-for-all-during-and-after-covid-19-pandemic/2021940/

Joshua Stern. *Introduction to Online Teaching and Learning*. Retrieved on April 17, 2020 from http://www.wlac.edu/ online/documents/otl.pdf

UGC notice. An Appeal for Inviting ideas/ suggestions for "Bharat Padhe Online campaign". Retrieved on April 16, 2020 from https://www.ugc.ac.in.

UGC notice. LET COVID 19 not stop you from learning – ICT initiatives of MHRD & UGC. Retrieved on April 16, 2020 from https://www.ugc.ac.in.

UNESCO. *COVID-19 Educational Disruption and Response*. Retrieved on April 14, 2020 from https://en.unesco.org/ covid19/ education response

UNESCO. *Distance learning solutions*. Retrieved on April 14, 2020 from https://en.unesco.org/covid19/educationresponse

UNICEF. Children at increased risk of harm online during global COVID-19 pandemic. Retrieved on April 16, 2020 from https://www.unicef.org/turkey/en/press-releases/children-increased-risk-harm- online-during-global-covid-19-pandemic

Wiesemes, R. & Wang, R. (2010). "Video conferencing for opening classroom doors in initial teacher education: sociocultural processes of mimicking and improvisation." *International Journal of Media, Technology and Lifelong Learning,* 6(1): 1-15.

World Bank. How countries are using edtech to support access to remote learning during the COVID-19 pandemic. Retrieved on April 16, 2020 from https://www.worldbank.org/ en/topic/edutech/brief/ how-countries-are-using-edtech-to-support-remote-learning-during-the-covid-19-pandemic

7

Teaching through the Electronic Media Especially in the Pandemic Period

Boni Dutta

Introduction

The year 2020 is a crucial year in the negative sense of the term. It witnessed the pandemic situation where people were forced to stay at home because of the virus known as Corona. The entire education system literally became stand still. On 11th February 2020, WHO announced a name for the new coronavirus disease as COVID-19. As lockdowns continue throughout the world, many individuals are heading online for help, especially educational institutions. E-learning is now the mandatory component of all educational institutions like schools, colleges, and universities in India and around the world due to the pandemic crisis, i.e. COVID-19. The consequence is that, it has flipped out the very offline teaching scenario at such locations. But yes, E-learning does provide us an opportunity towards effective teaching method that might bring out the best in students. It is nothing new but has become quite popular among the students all over the world particularly, in the lockdown period. Earlier, smart classes were used for dissemination of the syllabus, however, it was at the discretion of the educational institutions but now it is a compulsion.

The closure of educational institutions did significantly affect students, especially those belonging to the Economically Weaker Section (EWS) of the society. The majority of EWS students were unable to explore online learning resources due to lack of e-learning know-how and unavailability of required infrastructure including laptops, tablets, smartphone and internet. In India, (according to UNESCO survey) more than 15 lakh institutions are closed and about 25 crore of school students are not able to go to their schools. Out of these 25 crore students, about 80 per cent fall in EWS category. Even the teachers initially were unequipped to pull the students to the class or maintain the decorum of the same. Less than 15% of rural Indian households have Internet as opposed to 42% urban Indian households. A mere 13% of people aged above five in rural areas and just 8.5% of females could use the Internet. The poorest households cannot afford a smartphone or a computer. Though Governments, NGOs and other public-private organisations are trying to alleviate this serious deficiency.

Education, as a result, has largely moved online. There was a surge in the use of language apps, virtual tutoring, video conferencing tools, and online learning software in the last nine months. India, too, is witnessing an e-learning boom. Classes on Google Meet, Soom, WhatsApp and Skype are becoming the norm for students, parents and teachers. Yet, this abrupt transition to online hardly compensates for the absence of the classroom experience. There is also increased screen time for children, which is now but inevitable. There are also few parents who aren't comfortable with the technology themselves. So, their children, too, might look at it negatively. At times, classes also get disturbed due to Internet issues. Also, every teacher has a unique teaching style. Over a period, they would have built a rapport with the children. This is done through observing their body language in class or their interaction with their classmates. Further conducting large-scale, high-stakes examinations, was more complicated. Subjective examinations were reduced to objective tests on Google forms or may have extended to oral tests. Most board and entrance examinations have been either postponed or suspended, causing disruptions in the academic calendar. The students who are slated to appear for next year's board exams, for instance, have already lost instructional time.

In traditional classrooms, teachers can give students immediate face-to-face feedback. Students who are experiencing problems in the curriculum can resolve them quickly and directly either during the lecture or during the dedicated office hours. Personalised feedback has a positive impact on students, as it makes learning processes easier, richer, and more significant, all the while raising the motivation levels of the students. E-Learning, on the other hand, still tends to struggle with student feedback. Students completing regular assessments become dissatisfied when they experience a lack of personalised feedback. The traditional methods of providing student feedback don't always work in an E-Learning environment, and because of this, online education providers are forced to look towards alternative methods for providing feedback. Providing student feedback in an online setting is still a relatively unresearched topic area, and it might take a while for any specific strategies to become fully research-based and proven to be effective. The E-Learning methods currently practiced in education tend to make participating students undergo contemplation, remoteness and a lack of interaction. As a result, many of the students and teachers who inevitably spend much of their time online, can start experiencing signs of social isolation due to the lack of human communication in their lives. Social isolation coupled with a lack of communication often leads to several mental health issues such as heightened stress, anxiety, and negative thoughts. Lack of self-motivation among students continues to be one of the primary reasons why students fail to complete online courses. In traditional classrooms, there are numerous factors which constantly push students towards their learning goals. Face-to-face communication with professors, peer-to-peer activities, and strict schedules all work in unison to keep the students from falling off track during their studies. In the setting of an online learning environment, however, there are fewer external factors which push the students to perform well. In many cases, the students are left to fend for themselves during their learning activities, without anyone constantly urging them on towards their learning goals. Students taking E-Learning courses will find that they are often required to learn difficult materials in a comfortable home setting without any of the added pressure normally associated with traditional colleges. As a result, keeping up with regular deadlines during online studies can become difficult for those students who lack strong self-motivation and time management skills. E-Learning methods are proven to be highly effective at improving the academic knowledge of the students. However, developing the communicational skills of the students is an area often neglected during online lessons. Due to the lack of face-to-face communication between peers, students and teachers in an online setting, the students might find that they are unable to work effectively in a team setting. Neglecting the communicational skills of the students will inevitably lead to many graduates who excel in theoretical knowledge, but who fail to pass their knowledge on to others. Unfortunately, one of the biggest disadvantages of E-Learning continues to be cheating through various methods. Compared to on-campus students, online students can cheat on assessments more easily as they take assessments in their own environment and while using their personal computer. The students cannot be directly observed during assessments without a video feed, making cheat detection during online assessments more complicated than for traditional testing procedures. Additionally, without a proper identity verification system in place, students taking online assessments might be able to let a third party take the assessment instead of themselves, resulting in a wholly fraudulent test result.

References

E-students.org, thehindu.com, ndtv.com, weforum.org, globalgiving.org, edsys.in, e-learningforkids.org

R. Radha, K. Mahalakshmi, Dr. V. S Kumar, Dr. A R Saravana Kumar, "E-Learning during Lockdown of Covid-19 Pandemic, a Global Perspective," *International Journal of Control and Automation.*

Shivangi Dhawan, *Online Learning: A Panacea in the time of Covid-19 crisis.*

The Telegraph and Uttar Banga Sambad.

8

Implication of E-Learning in Teaching Methodology

Indranil Ghosh

Introduction

The learning activity involves the learner, the learning system to obtain knowledge in order to produce desired learning outcomes and satisfaction. The drivers or antecedents of the success of an e-learning system are the quality factors that are to be dealt with during the design and implementation of an e-learning system. If a learning management system has sophisticated technical features, it will enable the creating and delivering high quality content to the learners. Only self-motivated learners who have the ability to take up self-regulated learning can succeed in a technology based learning environment. Also a conducive learning environment supports success. All such quality concerns should be given due importance while developing and implementing a system. E-learning refers to computer based training that integrates technologies that support higher levels of interactivity. It connects people to appropriate learning resources. E-learning facilitates and enhances learning using the information and communication technology. The digital media and technology is used to deliver learning experiences that simulate the traditional classroom learning. E-learning services are provided through mobile technologies, personalised knowledge management and social networks. With the help of these tools, learners explore learning objects, generate and share ideas with other learners and ultimately gain new knowledge. The salient features of the e-lessons include ownership of the faculty, use of the visuals and participatory teaching methodologies, flexibility and scope for improvisation along with the use of basic principles of learning. The lessons are developed in house with the total involvement of all the faculty members. The extensive use of visuals and animations ensured, the teaching becomes easy and interesting particularly for the dull and mediocre students. The primary idea behind the development of e-lessons is to bring about a shift from the lecture-mode-of-teaching to learning with large scale participation of students. The e-lessons provide flexibility to the faculty to make changes and to bring in the local contexts so that the students can easily relate them to the subjects being taught and thus ensuring better retention of memory.

Uses of Basic Principles of E-Learning

The following basic principles of learning have been used in the preparation of e-lessons to ensure that the tea. Each of the e-lessons prepared explain the objectives of the lessons at the beginning of the lessons making it very clear in the minds of the students as to what they would learn at the end of each lesson. The e-lessons provide flexibility to the faculty to make changes and bringing the local contexts so that the students can relate them to the subjects being taught and thus improving better retention of memory. The e-lessons were also prepared keeping in mind the questions appeared in the previous examinations so that the course materials contain answers to these questions as well. This would help students in preparing more effectively for the examinations and would improve the overall results. A quis in the form of "objective questions" has been designed. In the e-lesson, the faculty can use this as an evaluation at the end of each topic. This would help in providing feed back to the faculty as well as students, accordingly if needed they can revise the subject. The e-lessons thus prepared, must be used and improved with constant upgradation. The faculty members should fill the feedback form for the e-lessons taught which is available on the web site of the department. The feedback would help in improving the quality of lessons for the future. The feedback from the faculty along with suggestions for improvement would be compiled. Based on the rating of the lessons and feedback, an expert committee would improve the e-lessons for future use. Asynchronous e-learning, the method of teaching in which there will not be any teacher available physically but only e-lessons and support materials will be available on the net. Essentially one-to-one teacher-student interaction will not be there in this system of teaching learning. Synchronous learning is a method wherein the teacher is available either physically or online to clarify the doubts or queries that are raised by the students thus facilitating one-to-one interaction during the learning process.

Trends of Corporate E-Training

Evolution of the Information and Communication technology is conventional these days and it is revolutionising every aspect of business. Innovative methods of producing, selling, financing and resourcing are making the industry highly dynamic. The shift from a product based economy to a knowledge based economy has increased the need for the employees to be equipped with all the latest technologies and new knowledge to solve complex issues in the work place. It has become imperative for organisations to utilise knowledge for creating new and better products as to confront domestic and global competition. Training has advanced from being just a means for employee skill development, to a platform for devising strategies to rationalise business goals. A steadfast training platform has to be sandwiched in between rigid schedules of geographically separated teams. The learning content has to be mastered by the employees in an environment characterised by time and cost pressures. In such a constricted predicament, e-learning stands as an obvious solution, as it offers diverse education opportunities to the trainees. It efficaciously connects education with employment. E-learning has improved the quality of teaching and learning. Employee training is the systematic acquisition of attitudes, skills and rules resulting in improvement in job performance. Companies use e-learning platform for corporate training for a number of reasons – self paced, cost effective and time saving, large target audience, Higher knowledge retention, easy course tracking and encourages sharing. Learners have control over the learning environment and hence they can learn at their convenient pace and determine their own learning schedules. E-learning enables companies to provide an opportunity for on-demand learning to every employee, thereby saving training cost and time. Organisations may achieve the benefits of cost efficiency, better accessibility and increased flexibility by implementing e-learning. As organisations become more competitive and the need for highly skilled employees increases, there is a greater need for a responsive and innovative workforce. A key factor in the ability of an organisation to create a climate for the rapid acquisition of new knowledge and skills is the provision of planned and formal training. One such form of planned training to have emerged in recent years is e-learning. E-learning is a valuable training and development solution, and has greatly impacted the way training initiatives are delivered and how learning occurs in many organisations.

E-Learning Initiatives in India

India has taken lessons from the success of the e-way in the West and today the grim educational picture is being replaced by e-governance's classroom, e-tutorials. It is a matter of pride for the country in general and agencies in particular for the popularisation of the Mission mode programmes on e-governance. The major advantage of e-learnings that it is self-paced and learning is done at the learner's pace. The content can be repeated until the trainee understands it. E-learning is interactive too. More and more working professionals would be interested in learning the e-way because of flexibility that e-learning offers. The future of e-learning is bright. However, one of the problems with e-learning in India is the lack of course content, especially outside the mainstream focus areas of IT education, English-language content and tutorial-like courses. However, there is significant knowledge retention. High quality e-learning solutions are being developed in India with the right technology and industry support in sectors as distinct as steel,

IT, automobiles, cement and telecom. Industry watchers estimate that because of its advantages, India is bound to grow in stature as the hub for e-learning programmes. Interestingly, many organisations are booming up here in India for providing e-classes. Places like Mumbai and Bangalore are becoming prominent centres for providing e-tutorials. It's booming but the big question is what is the future of e-learning? Everyone be it educators, parents or students has this question in mind but no one is able to answer. To check it out, its imperative to look to the trends concerned with e-learning, which are already taking control in our world. It seems imperative that e-learning would coexist with other technologies and ways of acquiring knowledge. And as soon as low cost PCs would be made available and broadband will penetrate deeper, particularly in rural areas, there are chances that e-learning will strengthen. Over the past five years, the Ministry of Human Resource Development has been busy attaining the goal of making education accessible to every child, particularly among the marginalised sections in the rural areas. Furthermore, the government is roping in as many colleges as possible under the ambit of the University Grants Commission to upgrade their quality. The UGC and AICTE are also pursuing various measures to lure fresh graduates into research and teaching professions. Integration of ICT in education will give an impetus to our efforts to attain our target of increasing our gross enrolment ratio by widening the reach of education to the remote and marginalised areas of our country. The role of Open and Distance Learning systems, which have accepted and integrated ICT in their functioning and outreach, particularly finds mention here. The government needs to stimulate a learning culture and e-leaning must become a policy issue. In every sector, efforts are normally made to bring improvement and while searching for ways and means to improve the education sector, e-learning using ICT tools has been found to be greatly useful for bringing a substantial change in the student – teacher interaction and thus achieving a quantum jump in the learning process. As such Govt. of India is encouraging the use of ICT tools in all areas of education vis. learning, teaching, sharing of knowledge etc.

Role Of Information Communication Technology (ICT) In Improving The Technical Education: The Twenty First century, a Century of Information and Communication Technology has influenced all aspects of human life. Its influence is felt in many endeavours such as online banking, online shopping, telecom, online ticketing, travel & tourism, online exams, online tax payment, online utility bill payments like, telephone, electricity, property tax, water tax and instant transfer of money. ICT has made inroads into the education sector also. In the 1980s, it was used for student information and student records, exams and fee particulars. It is now being extended to several other areas including teaching and content delivery. Alongside efforts are also made for improving the quality of education by implementing the modem ICT tools and technique. Some of these are updating the curriculum, starting new courses, faculty development, new methods of teaching learning etc. Technical Education plays a vital role in national development. The growth of any industry depends on technical manpower. For any industry to flourish, it requires high quality manpower. Every industry requires technicians at the middle level with adequate knowledge and skills in large numbers. Technicians with the right skill will be able to operate machinery efficiently and can contribute a lot to the production. If there is a mismatch between the skills possessed by the workers and the requirements of the industry, then the industry may not be able to achieve the targeted productivity and quality output.

Significance of the Study

For introducing, e-lessons, the state has harnessed vast resources. Moreover, like any new project this also went through several teething problems like shortage of manpower, infrastructure, needs networking of systems, design corrections, training needs of the personnel involved in the project etc. All this needed some amount of expertise in addition to the physical resources. Further, it is to be noted here that e-learning is a new concept in the Indian context and it is more so in the case of school education. Therefore, there are good amount of possibilities that even the faculty may not utilise the e-lessons provided for teaching in the classroom. In this background only, a detailed study has been planned to picturise the status of implementation as well as the problems faced during and after the implementation and finally evaluate the effectiveness of learning by the students. All these issues can be analysed and facts regarding the implementation can be brought out only through a study. It is to be noted that this e-lesson mode of teaching has been introduced in a short span of time and therefore is the necessity to study the associated problems and find solutions to them for further improving the effectiveness and output.

Conclusion

Employee training is the systematic acquisition of attitudes, skills and rules resulting in improvement in job performance. Companies use e-learning platform for corporate training for a number of reasons – self paced, cost effective and time saving, large target audience, Higher knowledge retention, easy course tracking and encourages sharing. Learners have control over the learning environment and hence they can learn at their convenient pace and determine their own learning schedules. E-learning enables companies to provide an opportunity for on-demand learning to every employee, thereby saving training cost and time. Organisations may achieve the benefits of cost efficiency, better accessibility and increased flexibility by implementing e-learning. As organisations become more competitive and the need for highly skilled employees increases, there is a greater need for a responsive and innovative workforce. A key factor in the ability of an organisation to create a climate for the rapid acquisition of new knowledge and skills is the provision of planned and formal training. One such form of planned training to have emerged in recent years is e-learning. E-learning is a valuable training and development solution, and has greatly impacted the way training initiatives are delivered and how learning occurs in many organisations.

References

Albers, S. (2010). "PLS and success factor studies in marketing", In: V. Esposito Vinsi, Chin, WW, Henseler, J & Wang, H (Eds), *Handbook of partial least squares: Concepts, methods, and applications.* Berlin: Springer (in print).

Alhendawi, K.M. & Baharudin, A.S. (2013). "The mediating role of web user satisfaction on information quality, service quality and the effectiveness of web-based information system," *Journal of Convergence Information Technology*, vol. 8, no. 12, p. 29.

Caporarello, L. & Sarchioni, G. (2014). "E-learning: the recipe for success", *Journal of e-Learning and Knowledge Society*, vol. 10, no. 1.

Carmines, E.G. & Seller, R.A. (1979). *Reliability and validity assessment*, vol. 17. Sage publications, India.

Geisser, S. (1974). "A predictive approach to the random effect model", *Biometrika*, vol. 61, no. 1, pp.101-107.

Hair, J. F., Black, W. C., Babin, B. J., & Anderson, R. E. (2009). *Multivariate Data Analysis 7th Edition*, Pearson Prentice Hall.

Islam, A.N. (2011). "The determinants of the post-adoption satisfaction of educators with an e-learning system," *Journal of Information Systems Education,* vol. 22, no. 4, p. 319.

Kim, K, Trimi, S, Park, H, & Rhee, S. (2012). "The impact of CMS quality on the outcomes of e-learning systems in higher education: an empirical study," *Decision Sciences Journal of Innovative Education,* vol. 10, no. 4, pp. 575-587.

Mohammadi, H. (2015). "Factors affecting the e-learning outcomes: An integration of TAM and IS success model," *Telematics and Informatics,* vol. 32, no. 4, pp.701-719.

Norman, P. M. (2004). "Knowledge acquisition, knowledge loss, and satisfaction in high technology alliances," *Journal of Business Research,* vol. 57, no. 6, pp. 610-619.

Roca, J.C., Chiu, C.M. & Martínes, F.J. (2006). "Understanding e-learning continuance intention: An extension of the Technology Acceptance Model," *International Journal of human-computer studies,* vol. 64, no. 8, pp. 683-696.

Selim, H. M. (2007). "Critical success factors for e-learning acceptance: Confirmatory factor models," *Computers & Education,* vol. 49, no. 2, pp. 396-413.

Yusuf, M.O. and S.A. Onasanya, (2004), "Information and Communication Teleology (ICT) and Teaching in Tertiary Institutions", In *Teaching in Tertiary Institutions, Ogunsakin,* E.A. (Ed.). Faculty of Education, University of Ilorin, Ilorin, Nigeria, pp. 67-76.

9

Impact of the COVID-19 Pandemic on Education

Jayeeta Roy

Introduction

The COVID-19 pandemic situation has affected the educational system worldwide. In an attempt to reduce the spread of COVID-19 most governments around the world have temporarily closed educational institutions. Currently approximately 1.077 billion learners are affected due to school closures. According to UNICEF monitoring, 53 countries are currently implementing local closures, impacting about 61.6 percent of the world's student population. 72 countries' schools are currently open. This is the scenario around the world.

Due to this pandemic situation, learners are facing different problems in India especially rural areas. The government of India has introduced lots of educational facilities, still education is a challenging in this third world country. It is very true that education is an important factor in the economic development of any country. Then the question is why do we face the challenges? Indian since the early days of independence has always focused on improving the literacy rate in our country. I have mentioned earlier also nowadays the government provides many programs to promote Primary and Higher Education in India.

India is a country where 60 percent of its population lives in villages or rural areas. Socioeconomic status is the most important issue in the contemporary world, specifically in the developing world. Many programs and policies have been implemented to improve the socioeconomic growth in rural areas. But economic status could not develop in rural areas. Another important objective of this paper is to understand the problems and challenges in rural areas. The major problems are poverty, illiteracy, unemployment, homelessness, malnourishment, violence and so and so forth. Lack of basic infrastructure like schools, colleges, hospitals, sanitation etc. So these are the basic regular problems in rural areas.

We need to know first, after this COVID-19 pandemic situation, what are the social conditions in those areas? Migration has also become common with the village people or rural people. We know it very well there was a time when the village did not leave his village for earning a livelihood. They were searching their jobs in urban areas for live their life well. During this pandemic what is the effect for these people, we know it well. Simple thing is that these 60% population of India those who live in remote areas, they live from hand and mouth. They can't even think to secure their future.

So most important objective of this paper is, how can we think about the e-learning process? Yes, it is very true in this situation we can't provide any offline mode education but what about those students who can't take any online facilities. It is a very regular case, mostly teacher face that some students haven't internet connection, not even smart phone. This pandemic situation effects our social, economic life. We have been suffering from this pandemic for 7 to 8 months.

This is a crucial time for the educational sectors – nursery school admission, board examination, entrance examination of various universities, competitive examinations and so and so forth, are all held during this pandemic period. There is no immediate solution to stop the outbreak of Coronavirus. For that reason there is no surety to open the schools, colleges and universities in normal way. Because these are the places, it is a big chance to spread this disease abnormally. It'll be the major risk with our future generations. It is very true that the structure and program of schooling and learning, including all methodologies like teaching, assessment, examination were the very first to be affected by these closures. Only some private schools could adopt online teaching methods. Like they can afford smart devices, internet facilities so and so forth. On the other hand low income private and government schools and others have completely shut down for not having access to e-learning programs. The learners of these group missed all opportunities for learning. Even they and their family members have not taken any healthy meals during this time. It is a hard truth, for these things, there create economic and social stress. This pandemic situation has disrupted the educational areas as well as country's economic future. Recent graduates in India are facing problems withdrawal of job offers from corporate areas. How much they can feel the pressure? Besides this, a large number of Indian students enroll in universities abroad, especially in countries worst affected by this pandemic. We just can't even imagine the mental pressure of those students.

It is the biggest transformation from chalk and talk learning to digital learning. We have to adopt digital learning process. One thing is that immediate measures are essential to ensure continuity of learning in government schools, colleges and universities. There is only one source through which we can continue the learning process that is nothing but e-learning program. Many institutions have shifted their academic performance into virtual platforms. All stages of education from pre-primary to university level have started online education as an alternative to ordinary face to face classes. Accordingly many stakeholders like government and private organisations are trying to give their best performances for e-learning program in this competition market. In this pandemic time they always encourage to teachers to use online apps and platforms to the optimum level. These organisations are providing training facilities for teachers. Moreover, efforts are being made by both government and private organisations and companies to support the school, college and university system to make a smooth transition to the digital world. Stakeholders are organising some counseling sessions for teachers, students and parents. Recently the Central government has launched the PM e-VIDYA platform, with 12 new DTH channels, every class to reach out to all status of society.

However, these alternative medium has also brought some social inequalities. These digital initiatives can balance the educational system during this pandemic. But there arises another issue digital divide is affecting the work and role of the government and private organisations as they are facing challenges. Millions of migrant labors are in native places. Both central government and state governments will have to take proper decision not only for labors' employment but for the education of their children too.

Especially Indian migrant workers during the COVID-19 pandemic have faced various difficulties in their lives. Industries and work places shut down due to the lockdown all over the country, migrant labors had to deal with the loss of income, insufficient foods and uncertainty about their future. As a result many of them and their family members walking back home, with no meal and transport due to the lockdown. At that time the Central and state governments took various measures to help them and arranged meal and transport for them. Approximately more than 500 migrant workers died for road and rail accident, denial of medical care, starvation, anxiety, suicide, exhaustion, unkindness of police and so and so forth during this lockdown period.

According to research mostly migrant workers are daily wage earners and working in the manufacturing and construction industries. These industrialists are frequently denied to serve their adequate nutrition, housing, sanitation, healthcare and others. Can we imagine the troubles of migrants during this period? From this situation how do they even think about e-learning solutions?

Conclusion

Students and teachers have their own struggles to use their online platforms. Due to financial condition students are not able to access the internet. There are some people who can't even use electronic gadgets and laptops, smart phone, computer, radio and T.V. The aim of the constitution of India is to provide equal educational opportunities to all citisens irrespective of caste, class, gender and religion. According to Constitution of India article 29(1) provides for equal access to educational institutions maintain by the State without any discrimination on grounds of religion, race, caste, language and others. Similarly Education Act or Right of Education Act (RTE) is an Act the Parliament of India enacted on 4 August 2009,which describes that all children from 6 to 14 years in India receives quality elementary education irrespective of their economic or caste background. However all the efforts, rules and regulations of the government for urban areas where people are economically stable and they can adopt e-learning solution. But what about those people meal for all family members.

References

"Bihar girl, who cycled down 1200 km carrying father, to be called for trial by cycling federation". *The Hindu*. Press Trust of India. 23 May 2020. ISSN 0971-751X. Retrieved 27 May 2020.

"Coronavirus | 5 trains cancelled in Kerala over NOC". *The Hindu*. 5 May 2020. ISSN 0971-751X. Retrieved 9 May 2020.

"Coronavirus lockdown | Over 60,000 people have registered on Delhi govt portal to go back home". *The Hindu*. Press Trust of India. 15 May 2020. ISSN 0971-751X. Retrieved 18 May 2020.

"Gujarat lockdown: Protests by migrant workers erupt again in Surat, this time over quality of food being served". *The Financial Express*. 16 April 2020. Retrieved 19 May 2020.

"India to Provide Free Food Grains to Millions of Migrant Workers". *The New York Times*. Reuters. 14 May 2020. ISSN 0362-4331. Retrieved 16 May 2020.

"Not allowed to enter UP after walking 200 km, migrants protest". *The Tribune*. 18 May 2020. Retrieved 19 May 2020.

Abi-Habib, Maria; Yasir, Sameer (29 March 2020). "India's Coronavirus Lockdown Leaves Vast Numbers Stranded and Hungry". *The New York Times*. ISSN 0362-4331. Retrieved 13 May 2020.

CDC COVID-19 Response Team. *Characteristics of health care personnel with* COVID-19: United States, February 12 – April 9, 2020.

Centres for Disease Control and Prevention. How COVID-19 spreads. 2020 [internet publication].

Coronaviridae Study Group of the International Committee on Taxonomy of Viruses. *The species severe acute respiratory syndrome-related coronavirus: classifying 2019-nCoV and naming it SARS-CoV-2*. Nat Microbial.

Dutta, Anisha (2 June 2020). "198 migrant workers killed in road accidents during lockdown: Report". *Hindustan Times*. Retrieved 13 June 2020.

Ernst, J. 2020 *US migrant deportations risk spreading coronavirus to Central America*. The Guardian, 12 March.

Fredrick, Oliver (3 June 2020). "Lucknow's 'lifeline' to Mumbai back on track". *Hindustan Times*. Retrieved 4 July 2020.

National Institutes of Health. Coronavirus disease 2019 (COVID-19) treatment guidelines. 2020 [internet publication].

Pandey, Alok (28 June 2020). ""Coronavirus Better Than Hunger," Say UP Migrant Workers Going Back To Work". *NDTV*.com. Retrieved 4 July 2020.

Pandey, Vikas (20 May 2020). "The Covid-19 migrants who never got home". *BBC News*. Retrieved 23 May 2020

Rashid, Omar; Anand, Jatin; Mahale, Ajeet (4 April 2020). "India coronavirus lockdown | Migrant workers and their long march to uncertainty". *The Hindu*. ISSN 0971-751X. Retrieved 18 May 2020.

Singh, Kanika (6 April 2020). "Coronavirus outbreak: Ensuring water, hygiene facilities for migrant labourers can safeguard millions stranded during shutdown". *Firstpost*. Retrieved 16 May 2020.

Srivastava, Roli; Nagaraj, Anuradha (29 April 2020). "As migrant workers struggle for lockdown aid, India seeks to count them". Reuters. Retrieved 17 May 2020.

Vadlamudi, Swathi (19 April 2020). "Sans Aadhaar, no ration for migrants". *The Hindu*. ISSN 0971-751X. Retrieved 19 May 2020.

World Health Organisation. *Clinical management of COVID-19: interim guidance*. 2020 [internet publication].Full text external link opens in a new window

World Health Organisation. Transmission of SARS-CoV-2: implications for infection prevention precautions – scientific brief. 2020 [internet publication].

10

Digital Learning: A New Technique in the Indian Education System

Joydeep Singh

Introduction

Digital Learning and Digital Education in India has progressed significantly with the advancement of innovation. India is one of the countries that are creating at an exponential rate as far as innovation is concerned. The ascent of the web has changed Indian lifestyle. Individuals like to do everything on the web; they shop on the web, work together on the web, make companions on the web, learn online and so on. While web based business being huge in online industry, online instruction and E-learning stand directly close to it. With the ever-expanding data accessible on the web and the incalculable number of online courses numerous individuals in India want to learn on the web.

In the current time, where innovation is quickly developing, instruction has likewise taken the help of ICT and now offers advantageous approaches to help increment the information, training and education status of individuals. E-learning stage gives anyplace, whenever simple access for up-degree of information and aptitudes.

Fascinating realities about Digital Learning in India

Owing to the coronavirus pandemic, the education sector is in crisis at the moment. Educational institutes are closed and most probably, they will remain closed through 2020 due to an increasing number of Covid-19 cases. This could even extend to 2021.

In this situation online education has come to the rescue of the cause of education. However there are several challenges of online education and the same needs to be fixed: –

Lack of Proper Study Room

Census 2011 tells us that 71 per cent of households with three or more members have dwellings with two rooms or less (74 per cent in rural and 64 per cent in urban areas). In such a situation how will the children avail education in an undisturbed ambience remain a huge question?

Inadequate Internet Penetration

According to National Sample Survey data for 2017-18, only 42 percent of urban and 15 percent of rural households had internet access, and only 34 per cent of urban and 11 per cent of rural persons had used the internet in the regular basis. These data clearly suggest that 2/3rd of the children will be left out of the online education process. The worst affected, as always, will be the marginalised, rural and poor population.

Slow Internet Speed

When it comes to online education, it is mostly about communicating with teachers directly through video calls or watching online video lectures, and both require high-speed and stable internet connection. In absence of adequate speed of the internet the whole idca will fail.

No Standard Policy

Digital education is not about videos of lectures on blackboards by teachers on the internet. It is about appropriate platforms, technology, tools, interactivity, creation, content and a lot more. We lack a proper policy on digital education, infrastructure, content, interaction and multiple languages.

Lack of Social Cohesion

Public educational institutions also play an exemplary role in social inclusion and relative equality. It is the place where people of all gender, class, caste, and community can meet without one group being forced to bow to others. This is an important learning in life which may not be supplemented by online education.

Teacher Training

Teachers look after the mental, emotional and social health of children in schools. Schooling is supposed to look after the emotional, social and behavioural health of children, which is diametrically opposite to social distancing. Teachers are not adequately trained to inculcate these learning's through online mediums.

Chances of Distraction are Very High

Understudies can without much of a stretch forget about their examinations in online instruction since there are no eye to eye talks and cohorts to remind you about tasks. Until and except if you keep yourself inspired it requires some investment to finish your course or relinquish your whole course.

Fraudulent Online Courses

There are numerous sites that offer online courses without the accreditation of any instructive power. Such courses won't be of any help in any form. So it is crucial to choose online courses carefully and after thorough research about them.

Cannot do Courses that Require Labs / Workshops

It is not possible to conduct a lab based course online.

Advantages of Digital Education

The online education market in India was worth $ 247 million in 2016, which is expected to grow about $ 1.96 billion by 2021. That is a compound annual growth rate of 52%. The number of users enrolled for various online learning courses is estimated to be 1.6 Million in 2016, which is expected to grow about 9.6 Million by the end of 2021. It is estimated that there is a 175% increase in the cost of classroom education, this gives online education more preferred because it is cost effective. Almost 48% populace in India between 15-40 ages bunches with high goals yet lower pay is a decent objective market for online training. Also, the adequacy of online divert is high in the more youthful segment. These elements unmistakably show the inclusion and future capability of online instruction in India.

Education beyond Boundaries

Digital content and e-learning can carry whole instructing modules to your doorstep through shrewd gadgets, making it feasible for understudies to keep pursuing finishing their training regardless of whether they hop off the way of customary learning. With a blast in less expensive information and gadgets, this method of learning demonstrates particularly viable in quest for advanced education or profession arranged abilities. Admittance to internet learning openings through far off classes, online courses and online foundations can accord equivalent learning occasions to understudies in Tier II and III urban communities just as rustic regions where gifted teachers in one's ideal field of study may not be accessible.

Personalised Learning

The coming of profound information investigation, Artificial Intelligence and Machine Learning, customised learning has become a substantial reality. These tech instruments permit empower distinguishing proof of understudy objectives – regardless of whether it is making sure about legitimacy, finding occupations or essentially gathering information – and make instructive substance to suit these objectives. This advances a genuinely customised approach toward learning. With the incorporation of edtech (Education-Technology) organisations and media in training, learning and instructing strategies have developed extraordinarily in their approach, style and substance.

Learning on the Go

Gadgets are a vital aspect of the adolescent's way of life today. From shopping to amusement and social associations, they look for everything on their fingertips and in a hurry. Their methodology toward training and learning is no exemption to this inclination. Advanced learning permits them to devour instructive substance in an arrangement they're more agreeable in and at a spot and setting based on their personal preference.

Affordability

The expense of advanced education in India is steep. By examination, particular online course are unquestionably more moderate. On the off chance that you factor in the expenses of moving to and living in a major city for understudies from Tier II and III urban communities, humble communities and country sones, proficient online courses don't cost a small amount of physical arrangements. It is consequently that India is quick developing as the second greatest market for MOOCs or open online courses, after the US. This new instructive unrest presents extraordinary occasion to enable the young to get to top notch training and preparing, at moderate value focuses, from the solace of their homes.

Job Readiness

The advanced education in India basically spins around making sure about a stable – preferably, well-paying – work. With simple admittance to e-learning stages and advanced substance, understudies can get to the correct sort of substance in an arrangement fit for their favored method of utilisation and be better prepared to meet this objective. For example, a similar educational program can be handily changed to suit scholarly and serious purposes in a practical way in the digital book design.

Future-Ready Education

Our surrounding is changing at an extremely quick pace, because of the consistent emissions in the innovation front. Tragically, the majority of the conventional discussions of learning – be it schools, schools or colleges – wind up falling behind with regards to fitting the course content according to the changing requirements. Furthermore, upgrading whole course of educational programs can be a moderately tedious cycle. In such a situation, customised online courses can be a bankable option in hoarding abilities that add to employability and is in accordance with the students' advantages.

Learn from anywhere, at any time

Since online training just requires a PC or a cell phone with a web association, understudies can adapt anyplace whenever. This adaptability causes working experts to seek after new courses without surrendering their positions. They can learn at ends of the week or in their available time. All the course materials are promptly accessible at the tip of understudy's finger.

Save Money and Time

Online instruction is considerably savvier than doing a normal nearby degree. It helps understudies who can't bear the cost of an ordinary advanced education to achieve their fantasy without spending a fortune on school instruction. Since you learn at your own time, it assists with sparing time too.

Learn at your own Pace

Everybody learns at an alternate movement. In a study hall where everybody showed together, numerous understudies think that it is hard to follow the exercises. This is a genuine hindrance of customary training. Online instruction tackles this issue. In online instruction all the course materials are given heretofore, understudies learn it by requiring some investment. Understudies can explain their questions by live visits or gatherings too.

Recognition of online Degrees

Online degrees are acknowledged by numerous organisations and businesses in India as long as it is licensed and endorsed by Distance Education Council (DEC) of India. A considerable lot of them are empowering their workers for getting on the web training too.

Access and Equity

Online access to similar learning resources offers the biggest advantage of all time access to all irrespective of their location, race, religion etc. i.e. it is barrier free and of same quality for all. It results in availability of learning opportunity to every human being on this planet earth without any discrimination and every society/ community/nation can march ahead for knowledge driven growth. Also, the different learners with different learning capability can access the learning resources as per their capability and limitations.

Affordable

Digital learning is quite affordable as the major cost is usually incurred in the initial phase of setting up of digital learning platform and populating it with learning resources while, the recurring cost of providing access, its maintenance and upgradation are not that large with the prevalent technological solutions. This less price for good quality learning resource with lot of ease makes the digital learning very attractive.

Better Engagement

The use of technology in digital learning has an attraction in presentation, and content, which is loved by the learners and leads to their better engagement. It also permits for use of gratification in learning, which really fascinates the learners

Mentoring

Conventional formal education system is limited contact type education system and the students fail to get the mentoring as per their need. The digital learning platforms are evolving with the facilitation for as and when mentoring of the learners with minimum response time. It also offers the capability to adapt to the individual's needs, personalised instructions, personalised doubts removal, and customised instruction based on analysis of learning capability of students and preserving it for continuous improvement using study behaviour and analytics.

Conclusion

In some cases, innovation turns into a reason for interruption to the student and clears path for the cheating in evaluation measures. It likewise prompts corruption of penmanship abilities of the students, as they don't get abundant composing openings. The substance creation measure includes innovation uphold too which implies that more intelligent capital is needed in the substance creation and the board when contrasted with the conventional training framework which prompts move in center from quality to the introduction arrangement and simple entry.

Further, it is exceptionally fundamental to have accreditation of advanced taking in asset from the viewpoint of its quality and validity, in light of the fact that any ill-advised substance when glided on web may have grievous ramifications of turning out unsatisfactory prepared human asset. The interoperability of computerised substance ought to be guaranteed so the various fragments learning assets stay intelligible. Security of electronic computerised content likewise should be guaranteed totally in order to forestall any misbehaviour.

It is apparent that the rich quality of computerised learning asset has part of potential; however simple interest for turning out to be advanced ought not to flout the advanced education framework from its centre subject of bestowing best quality instruction. Taking into account a portion of the downsides, there is a need to incorporate computerised learning with the traditional instructing learning cycles to enhance them and improve the nature of learning. Nonetheless, for the learning and advancement, which centers after helping individuals to become familiar with the aptitudes and get roused for upgrading profitability, computerised learning stages are acceptable due to their non-intrusive nature and the troubles of substance the executives, working interruptions and different coordination issues.

Further, it is very basic for the advanced education controllers of the nation to develop and uphold a total legitimate structure to keep vigil over the computerised content and computerised learning stages being made by various administrators with the business viewpoint and guarantee their accessibility after the essential accreditation affirmation.

References

https://eduxpert.in/online-education-india/

https://www.indiatoday.in/education-today/featurephilia/story/digital-learning-can-online-education-replace-the-school-classroom-in-india-1697474-2020-07-06

https://indianexpress.com/article/opinion/columns/digital-education-online-classes-learning-coronavirus-national-education-policy-6580744/

https://inc42.com/resources/future-trends-digital-education-india/

https://www.drishtiias.com/daily-updates/daily-news-editorials/digital-education-in-india

https://www.dqindia.com/digital-learning-can-solve-access-education-problem-indian-students/

11

Pandemic and its Consequences on Students' Mental Health

Nabanita Dutta

Introduction

The outbreak of Corona virus disease today has drastically changed the whole human life. Covid-19 has affected more than 4.5 million people worldwide. (WHO). In India the first affected case of Covid-19 was detected on 30th January 2020 in the state of Kerala and the affected has a travel history from Wuhhan, China (Wikipedia). Several States have also been affected. As the rate of spread is increasing day by day, Indian Government has announced lockdown in several phases. Under such circumstances all educational activities has been postponed. Thus pandemic Covid-19 has impacted significantly on students' life. Studies conducted during the COVID-19 period have found that students worldwide have been dramatically affected by the spread of COVID-19, after facing travel restrictions, physical distancing, isolation, and quarantining, as well as dormitory and border closure (Quacquarelli Symonds, 2020). All these changes affected mental health of students. Disturbances in the mental health not only have negative impacts on students' life but also have serious negative impacts on teachers, parents and other community members.

For college students, heightened levels of psychological distress and downstream negative academic consequences are prevalent under normal circumstances (American College Health Association, 2019). Quarantining at home and the closure of educational institutions were reported as major reasons for students feeling disconnected from society and their social circles (Killan, 2020). Postponement of examinations, change in daily routine, online learning are the various reasons that are sources of stress for the students. The students residing in rural areas are in a worse condition as they are deprived of modern technologies which hamper the cause of their online education. If such a situation persists for a long time there will be a significant decline in the system of higher education also.

Need of the Study

The outbreak of Covid-19 impacted drastically the world's student population. There is lockdown in every sector including education. Closure of educational institutions, physical distancing and home quarantine make students separated from the real world. As this is an unprecedented phenomenon, its effect is also devastating and widespread for which the whole world is suffering. In this condition there is an urgent need of studying mental health of students. Students today are going through different kinds of phase which they never encountered before. They are not getting any opportunity to visit schools and colleges. So they can't exchange their knowledge, share their thoughts and feelings with teachers and their friends. Students today are constraint from many different aspects. This confinement is creating loneliness among students. Small children are also missing their school days, story, singing and dancing classes. All these creating excessive mental strain on students' health which is also affecting their academic performance. So there is immediate need of studying mental health of students during Covid-19 pandemic.

Objectives

The present study has the following objectives: –

1. To know the impact of Covid-19 on mental health and academic performance of students.

2. To know the solutions in overcoming such pandemic situations

Methodology

The researcher has adopted qualitative study. A small interview of 100 college students was conducted over telephone and Google Meet.

Delimitation

This study is delimited with 100 students of Panskura Banamali College.

Impact of Covid-19 on Mental Health and Academic Performance of Students

A total of 100 college students participated in this study through telephone survey and Google Meet. Out of them 70% of the students reported that they are in severe psychological distress. The reasons are:

> Home isolation for a long period make most of the students frustrated. Majority told that as college is closed they are totally disconnected from their friends which lead them in a state of depression. Some students complained about that staying home for a long time make them bored, they feel monotonous. Many students at home are in mental pressure as excessive workloads are imposed upon them by parents and other family members. Therefore they don't get any extra time for other recreational activities. Some students told that in their family they are not free enough to express their feelings as elders are dominating upon them. Thus they experienced high level of frustrations and anxiety.

As lockdown period totally changed their life-style they could not concentrate on their studies. The examinations were also postponed and the actual date of examination is awaited. This situation makes most of the students nervous. Many students complained that results of the earlier semester have not been published yet. Therefore fear of academic failure is one of the major factors that increase their level of stress and anxiety. As classroom teaching has been shifted to online, students complained that they are not benefited with online learning. Internet connections are slow, especially in rural areas server remains down, some students could not afford smart phones due to financial problems so they are deprived from online classes. Some students reported that compared to online teaching, classroom learning is much more comfortable as there is direct interaction between teacher and students. In classroom they could get all materials, can ask questions if they have any doubts which is not always possible through online learning. Many students reported that in online classes they could not hear properly what teachers are saying, some are unable to connect with the link which teachers used to send before starting classes. Some students said that they are deprived of library reading. Other factors affecting their academic performance are time management, concentration, submitting online assignment in due time and low motivation.

Another 20% students reported moderate psychological distress. The said that:

> Home quarantine for a long time makes them bored. A change in lifestyle makes some students feel depressed. Due to lockdown they could not even visit to their nearby friends and relatives. Students are missing their college days, classroom teaching, interaction with peers and teachers, off time periods and extra-curricular activities which makes them somehow depressed. Some students who belong to low income families besides studying they have to earn something to support their family. They reported that some are not paid for months and some have lost their jobs during lock-down period which is the reason for their mental stress.

Some are very much anxious about their career as examinations are postponed and results are delayed. Not only that due to pandemic all competitive examinations have also been postponed. So not only academic but vocational career of some students are also getting affected. When asked about online learning 12% students reported that online classes provides an opportunity to save time and money and they devoted more time to their studies. It also increases their level of motivation. Remaining 8% spoke that they are facing several problems such as slow net connections, server down. Long duration of online classes make some students feeling sick. They have headache, drowsiness, backpain. Also some students could not join online classes due to excessive household work. So they are missing both online and offline teaching which affecting their mental development as well as well as academic performance. Some students are scared about online examinations. They said instead of online, offline examination is much better for them. Some students complained if two semesters examination would be held together how they could manage. Some students fear about year loss. All these factors affecting students' achievement level, they are unaware about their academic progress. Some students also reported that they are enjoying their free time through listening to music, watching movies, taking care of older people in home which provides them some kind of mental satisfaction.

Remaining 10 % students reported mild psychological distress. They said that though home quarantine makes them bored and lonely but somehow they are capable of managing the situations. They are enjoying their holidays. Lock-down period provides opportunities for doing extra-work. Some started preparing for next semester, others are busy in completing their assignment. Students belong to this category have positive attitude towards online learning as they see it is a good opportunity to overcome the stress of pandemic and also they don't have to go to colleges regularly. By sitting at home they are getting all teaching-learning materials. They also reported that during online teaching, apart from academic discussion they can share their pent-up feelings with teachers which provide them emotional support. Devoting extra time for study, preparing notes and materials helping them to improve their academic performance. Some students told that they are preparing for competitive examinations. When asked about examination they said they feel little bit tensed due to postponed of examination but somehow they can manage with both online and offline system.

They also reported lock-down periods enable them to utilise their leisure hours effectively. Girls are helping their mothers in cooking, cleaning and other household activities. Some boys told that online chatting with friends make them much relaxed. Most of the students are engaged in creative activities like drawing, painting, singing, recitation, etc. Some are performing Face book live to share their experiences during Covid-19. All these activities helping them in releasing their mental stress, anxiety and depression.

Findings

The findings of the current study include:

1. Most students experienced high level of anxiety and frustrations during Covid-19 period due to home isolation for a long time. Excessive workloads, domination of elders, separation from friends make them mentally disturbed.
2. Postponed of examinations, delay in results publication, impaired attention, lack of motivation and concentration are the factors that affecting students' academic performance.
3. Many students reported that absence of extra-curricular activities snatched their mental peace and happiness.
4. Half-payment and not getting salary for months are the reason for most students' mental tension.
5. Excessive home assignment, not completing and submitting assignment in due time are the reasons for anxiety and depression.
6. Most students reported negative attitudes towards online learning due to slow net connections, server down, some are not physically fit, and others are not habituated with this kind of learning. So many of them could not follow online teaching. All these highly affecting their academic level of achievement as they are totally deprived from classroom learning.

7. Very few students experienced mild level of anxiety. They said though they feel tensed in some situation, they are able to cope up with such tension producing situations by engaging themselves in academic as well as recreational activities. They reported positive attitudes towards online learning. Students noted online classes were effective and influential in increasing their level of motivation thus helping in improving their academic performance and mental health.

8. Covid-19 period also enables some students to utilise their leisure hours effectively by engaging themselves in various recreational activities.

To know the Solutions in overcoming such Pandemic Situations

Some solutions need to be provided to students in overcoming pandemic situations. These are: –

a) Parents should provide emotional support to their children. They must understand the psychology of every child especially at this crisis time and try to fulfill their various needs.

b) Students should be encouraged to read various kinds of story books and literature which will help them in upgrading their knowledge.

c) Students should be given more opportunities for online communication. Exchanging and sharing of knowledge, thoughts and ideas with teachers and friends may help in overcoming their mental stress of pandemic.

d) If possible, colleges may create websites for students' online library reading which will help them in developing regular study habits.

e) For science students teacher should suggest some experiments which can be done at home. This will help in upgrading their knowledge as well as improving their academic performance and experimental skills.

f) Some colleges are uploading educational materials on their websites which are helping students in learning, reading and completing their assignment.

g) Assignment should not contain only question-answer but also some project work should be given in order to secure good marks.

h) Online examination, mode of assessment, evaluation procedure should be made more flexible in order to overcome students' stress and anxiety.

i) Today many colleges are organising webinar on Covid-19 pandemic. Students should be encouraged to participate in such webinar so that they could know how to deal peacefully with such situations.

j) Students should be encouraged to utilise their leisure hours effectively by involving themselves in large number of creative activities like listening to music, essay writing, painting, singing, dancing, doing art and craft work to release their pent-up feelings,

k) Yoga is the best therapy for releasing all mental tension and anxiety. Online classes on Yoga education can be conducted which will provide both physical fitness and mental strength. Students should also practice meditation which will help them in increasing the power of attention, concentration and provide mental peace and happiness.

l) Offering online counseling to the needy students may prevent them to enter into the state of depression. Thus students will remain mentally healthy and they perform well in academic life.

Conclusion

Today's students are the future of tomorrow. The performance of the students depends on their mental health. The state of pandemic and its consequences is a source of massive stress that burdens individual students and impact their mental condition. Students are undergoing mental stress as till date there is no proven treatment to manage the novel Corona virus disease. Students experiencing high level of frustrations since everyday activities such as interacting with people in regular social situations became totally stopped. Closure of educational institutions and coaching classes made many students detached from their academic career for a long time. The economic consequences of pandemic lead to job losses mainly for rural students. Students overload and circumstances caused by Covid-19 can be best managed by offering flexibility in terms of opportunities to engage themselves in various teaching learning activities. Providing emotional and mental health support is one of the most important factors in protecting students from such pandemic. Students should be made aware of how to take care of their own mental health such as washing hands, using sanitiser, wearing mask before going out and maintaining social distancing. Also they should avoid warm handshake, personal greeting and close intimacy with every person for a long time. Appropriate Health Care Services should be made available for them for their own safety. Some coping strategies like Humanistic Therapy, Behavioral Therapy and Relaxation Therapy should be provided to students in order to overcome from stressful situations.

References

Agolla, J. E., & Ongori, H. (2009). "An Assessment of Academic Stress among Undergraduate Students: The case of University of Botswana." *Educational Research and Reviews, 4*(2), 063-070.

Arënliu, A., & Bërxulli, D. (2020). *Rapid assessment: Psychological distress among students in Kosovo during the COVID-19 pandemic.*

https://www.researchgate.net/publication/340262171 Rapid assessment Psychological distress among students in Kosovo during the Covid-19 Pandemic Accessed 22, April 2020.

Cohen, S., Kamarck, T., & Mermelstein, R. (1983). "A global measure of perceived stress." *Journal of Health and Social Behavior, 24,* 386–396

Grubic, Nicholas, Badovinac, Shaylea, Johri, Amer, M. (2020). "Student mental health in the midst of the Covid-19 pandemic: A call for further research and immediate solutions." *International Journal of*

Social Psychiatry, 1-2 retrieved from https://journals.sagepub.com/doi/full/10.1177/0020764020925108

Jena, Kumar, Pravat. (2020). "Impact of Covid-19 on Higher Education in India." *International Journal of Advanced Education and Research,* Volume 5; Issue 3; 2020; Page No (77-81) retrieved from: https://www.researchgate.net/publication/342277024_Impact_of_Covid-19_on_higher_education_in_India

Numan, A., & Hasan, S. S. (2017). "Effect of Study Habits on Test Anxiety and Academic Achievement of Undergraduate Students." *Journal of Research & Reflections in Education (JRRE), 11*(1).

12

Equity in Education: The Indian Scenario Especially during the Pandemic

Namit Lepcha

Introduction

The whole world is battling against Covid-19 pandemic, every aspects of human life has been gravely affected irrespective of socio-economic, political or demographic disparities. However the extent of pandemic impact and its measurability varies from people to people, country to country depending wholly on the concerned government's strategies and decisions. The human race has experienced drastic pandemonium that disrupted lifestyle globally. Many countries have closed the educational institutions to curb the further spread of virus. It has upset the educational process of the whole world. According to UN, the closure of schools and other learning spaces have impacted of 94 percent of world's students' population. The whole schooling process including learning and assessment methodologies have been transformed from chalk-talk to virtual learning. India traditionally embodied by prevalent disparities in every level of the society, the COVID 19 pandemic crisis is further exacerbating existing imbalance. Likewise the shift in the learning process also brought to forth such existing realities. Students belonged to poor family, rural areas, with disabilities or poor digital skills, are affected immensely. Disruption in education process also obstructed getting mid-day meal, furtherance in the drop-out rate and increased in rise of violence and abuse the issues like availability and affordability of resources and accessibility to the online class spawned a condition of digital divide in India. 'The crisis brought a deeper understanding of the digital divide and related equity gap'. Additionally ill equipped and weak educational infrastructure put forward the debate on the question of inclusive and equal accessibility of education in the country. Thus, in the scenario of shifting to online/virtual education, the question of equality and equity are undoubtedly crucial issues. In this paper an attempt has been made to highlight such issues taking into the account of Indian society and its inherent inequalities.

The Inherent Inequalities in Indian society

Indian society is evidently heterogeneous in nature. The socio-economic along with geographical diversity are intricately constructed and quite difficult to be found elsewhere. Rabindra Nath Tagore thus described India as world in miniature. India is a home of many religions like Islam (12%), Christianity (3%), Sikhism, Buddhism, and Jainism (3%) along with Hinduism in majority. Caste system has been historically prevalent in India. Untouchables, at the bottom in the caste hierarchy, are mainly socially and economically excluded. Besides, India's diversity is marked with the presence of geographically separated tribal groups. Tribal groups follow customs and practices that are not only distinct from mainstream Hinduism but also tend to vary from tribe to tribe. Thus India's diversity permeates with immense inequality and differences in the society. Poverty, Gender, Age, Language, physical appearance, demography are others variables that have caused more differences consequently inequality in society. Inequality also caused to unequal accessibility of resources. Resources are mainly 'economic capital, cultural capital and social capital and symbolic capital. These forms of capital overlap and can be converted into other'. In India social inequality and exclusion are facts of life... Social exclusion is not accidental but systematic. It is the result of structural features of society. Marginalisation, oppression, subjugation and exploitation continue to be interwoven with social stratification and social inequality in India. Education is a valuable resource of human development. It is an inevitable tool for nation building. Indian society and inherent inequalities resulted in discrepancy with regard to opportunity and access to education. The impact of parental socio-economic status on children's educational opportunity remained stable or widened. Hence, education system is characterised by stratification on the basis of class, caste, gender, region to name a few. There is no doubt that access to education in India is extremely unequal.

Covid-19 Pandemic and Equity in Education

Many countries closed educational institutions to curb the further spread of virus. According to UNESCO report as of 4th September 2020 approx 1.277 billion learners are affected and over 320 billion students have been affected in India. Both central and state governments, policy makers, educationists emphasised on technology driven or digital teaching/learning model. There is no doubt that in the present crisis situation e-learning ensures uniform platform and safe environment to both teachers and students. However India characterised by diversity and inherent inequalities, e-learning brought certain issues and concerns. The CAG report on education pointed out various discrepancies such as teacher – pupil ratio, poor planning and execution, low utilisation of funds, drop out, poor infrastructure etc. Report also points out the irregularities and corruption in the implementation of RTE Act. Indian education system is third largest in the world besides USA and China. The Covid pandemic has not only highlighted but also deepened the existing abysmal condition in India. The government has initiated several e-learning measures to ensure the smooth and continuous flow of learning process. Some of the few initiatives or projects are as follows –

- Swayam – online courses for school and higher education, National Digital library,
- FOSSEE – free/Libre and open source software for education,
- e-gyan kosh – to store and share the digital learning resources,

- epathsala, Diksha – national platform for teachers and learners,
- Sakshat – educational portal for all education and learning related needs of students, teachers and learners. It also provides latest news, press release etc.

These technology driven measures however have revealed all the prevailing inequalities in India. Accessibility of internet or electricity, lack of infrastructure, connectivity and digital capabilities and others several issues exposed the potential of digital learning. According to National Sample Survey report of 2017-18 only 24% of household have the internet facility. 15% of rural household and 42% of urban household have access to internet service. The vast gender gap has been revealed by Internet and Mobile association of India (2019). 67% of men accessed internet whereas only 33% of women accessed internet. Electricity is vital for accessing any resource. So far as electricity is concerned according to Ministry of Rural Development 2017-18, 16% of India's household received one to eight hours electricity, 33% household received nine to ten hours electricity and only 47% received more than twelve hours electricity. Thus income, socio-economic factors, age are determinants of access to internet; consequently access to digital learning. Additionally ill equipped and weak educational infrastructure put forward the debate on the question of inclusive and equal accessibility of education. The present pandemic crisis and consequently change in the learning process further worsens the situation.

Incidents of students' suicide in Kerala, Punjab, Assam, and Tripura due to inability to attend online class are some of the gloomy pictures of technology driven learning. It has also laid financial burden on poor families as they are forced to sell jewellery and cattle to buy smart phones. Children with disability are facing more difficulties with regard to accessing devices, absence of software and staying connected both physically and psychologically. They need special care and resources which are mostly unaffordable and not easily available in present situation. Students also trekked distances to connect with internet network for online classes. Gender inequality and increase in child labour are other consequence of shutting down of school and shifting to virtual class. Many poor girl students were forced to leave school and get married. Students have been disproportionately affected with the shutting down of school in general and particularly change in teaching method. Thus the question of equity in education has become crucial in the context of new teaching/ learning method. The immediate redressal of all these issues has become concern of all. The accomplishment of education through virtual teaching undoubtedly depends on the infrastructure, availability and affordability of resources and digital literacy. Simultaneously, the contemplation of parents, teachers and students also could not be ignored at all.

Conclusion

In conclusion, to fill the gap created due to shifting in learning process, it is imperative to consider some measures;

- Government along with other actors like service provider, NGOs should work together to ensure the smooth and efficient functioning of education process.
- Manufactures of indigenous devices and gadgets in low cost should be encouraged, to address issues of affordability and accessibility.
- Furthermore teachers have to be equipped with technological as well as psychologically to confront any unprecedented future development. Both students and teachers need to be motivated to adopt new measures of learning process.

References

UN Policy Brief: Education During Covid-19 and beyond, Aug 2020.

(UNESCO, international commission on the Futures of education, “Education in a post COVID19world: nine ideas for action”2020, https://undesdoc.unesco.org/ark:/48223/pf0000373717

Bourdian, P. (1986). 'The Form of Capital' in *Handbook of Theory and Research for Sociology of Education*, Edited. By Richardson John, NewYork: Greenwood

hppts://insightonindia.com/wp-content/2013/08/ Indian society retrieved on 17/09/20

NSS Survey Report 2017-18

Internet and Mobile association of India 2019

Ministry of Rural Development 2017-18

www.indiatvnews.com

www. tribuneindia.com

www. hindustan times.com

www. ndtv.com

13

Challenges of Higher Education System in the Covid-19 Situation

P. Ravi Kumar and **P. N. Lakshmi Shanmugam**

Introduction

Nationwide lockdown was implemented on 24th March 2020 which was extended until 17th May 2020 by the Prime Minister. This lockdown was carried over to restrict the spread of Corona virus. As per the report of UNESCO, Covid-19 has affected almost 68% of total world's student population as per the data taken during 1st week of June 2020. Outburst of Covid-19 has impacted about 1.2 billion students and youths across the world by school and university closures. Several countries have also implemented restricted closures impacting millions of additional learners. In India, more than 32 crores of students have been affected by the various limitations and the nationwide lockdown for Covid-19 (Wikipedia). The educational institutions are still wary of lifting closures in order to minimise the reach of the disease. This has affected their core efforts directed toward teaching, learning, and conducting research. As a solution, educational institutions have planned to keep the remote/online learning completely. Though, both teachers/students and educational institutions look abundant other difficulties connected to technology, quality of online learning, financing, and available infrastructure. How does higher education sector be ready for a crisis? How do they deal with the concerns related to the quality of online learning and digitalised set of courses? How do we face the problems of diversity and inclusion? It is important to address these lawful questions by going beyond short-term remedies. This opinion article shortly adds to the conversations surrounding the problems faced by higher education forum and potential solutions to reduce these issues.

Impact of Education during Pandemic

Millions of students have increased to study in abroad. The report meant that India has the largest source of international students in the world. It has destabilised the education sector. Covid-19 has created challenges (Pravat, 2020). Due to that activities like admission, examinations, entrance exam, competitive exams conducted by different boards/schools/colleges/universities have been postponed. The severe impact of COVID-19 has traumatised the world greatly. Additional, the superior part of the Governments across the world have quickly closed academic establishments trying an effort to embrace the unfold of the COVID-19 pandemic. In India as effectively, the federal government as a facet of the nationwide lockdown has closed each academic institution, as a result of which, learners going from school-going kids to postgraduate college students, are affected.

These nationwide closures are disturbing over 91% of the pupils around the world. UNESCO is supporting international locations of their efforts to moderate the quick impact of faculty closures, especially for extra weak and poor communities, and to facilitate the consistency of training for all via distant studying. The UNESCO information estimates that the Covid pandemic will unfavorably have an effect on over 290 million college students throughout 22 international locations. The UNESCO estimates that round 32 crores college students are affected in India, incorporating these in faculties and faculties. (indialegallive)

"The Centre for Monitoring Indian Economy's estimates on unemployment shot up from 8.4% in mid-March to 23% in early April and the urban unemployment rate to 30.9%. There is a strong need to evolve a comprehensive strategy for the higher education sector to handle the current demand of the students for higher studies in India. Further, immediate measures are required to mitigate the effects of the pandemic on job offers, internship programs, and research projects. *In this critical time*, a well-rounded, resilient and effective educational practice is needed for the capacity building of human resources with strong technical skills and strong research potential. This, in turn, will drive the employability, productivity, health, and well-being of graduate/undergraduate students in the decades to come, and ensure the overall progress of India." This answer was given in an interview with Dr KS Dasgupta, who was an Indian Scientist and Academician, for the question, "Recent graduates in India are fearing withdrawal of job offers from the corporates because of the current situation. What do you have to say about that?"

Approaches of Higher Education during Covid-19 in India

The government has provided with e-learning program. Few technology related companies have tried to influence the time by providing free on-line lessons or engaging limits on e-learning modules. These measures have been utilised with great response by college students with some new companies witnessing as extreme as 25% uptick in e-learning. Distant studying appears a viable reply for college kids throughout this time as they provide useful and reasonably rated entry to classes.

E-learning additionally comes as an attention-grabbing and interactive various as in association with classroom teaching.

Some of the digital initiatives of UGC & MHRD for higher education during COVID-19 are pointed as below:

- e-GyanKosh (http://egyankosh.ac.in/) is a National Digital Repository to store and share the digital learning resources which is developed by the Open and Distance Learning Institutions of India. Items in eGyanKosh are protected by copyright, with all rights reserved by Indira Gandhi National Open University (IGNOU).

- Gyandarshan (http://www.ignouonline.ac.in/gyandarshan/) is a web based TV channel dedicated to educational and developmental requirements for Open and Distance Learner. A web-based TV channel dutiful to educational and developmental needs of the society
- Gyandhara (http://ignouonline.ac.in/Gyandhara/) is an internet audio counselling service offered by IGNOU. It is a web radio where students can listen to the live discussions by the teachers and experts on the topic of the day and interact with them through telephone, email (gyandhara@ignou.ac.in) and through chat mode.
- Swayam provides Massive Open Online Courses (MOOCs) with 140 universities approved credit transferfeature. Swayam Prabha provides high quality educational programs through 32 DTH channels transmitting educational contents. e-PG Pathshala (https://epgp.inflibnet.ac.in/) is for postgraduate students. Postgraduate students can access this platform for e-books, online courses and study materials. The details of these three digital plat forms are described by the author in the previous paper (Pravat, 2020b).
- e-Adhyayan (e-Books) is a platform that provides 700+ e-Books for the Post-Graduate courses. All the e-Books are derived from e-PG Pathshala courses. It also facilitates play-list of video content.
- e-Pathya (Offline Access) is one the verticals of e-PG Pathshala which is software driven course/content package that facilitates students pursuing higher education (PG level) in distance learning as well as campus learning mode. It also facilitates offline access.
- National Digital Library of India (NDLI) (https://ndl.iitkgp.ac.in/) is a repository of e-content on multiple disciplines for all kinds of users like students (of all levels), teachers, researchers, librarians, library users, professionals,

differently-abled users and all other lifelong learners. It is being developed at Indian Institute of Technology Kharagpur. It is designed to help students to prepare for entrance and competitive examinations, to enable people to learn and prepare from best practices from all over the world and to facilitate researchers to perform inter-linked exploration from multiple sources. It is a virtual repository of learning resources with a single-window search facility. It is also available to access through mobile apps.

- e-Yantra (https://www.e-yantra.org/) provides hands on experience on embedded systems. It has about 380 Lab and made 2300+ colleges benefited.
- FOSSEE (https://fossee.in/) is short form for Free/Libre and Open Source Software for Education, which is developed to promote open source software for education as well as professional use.
- Virtual Labs (http://www.vlab.co.in/) has developed web-enabled curriculum based experiments designed for remote operation. It has over 100 Virtual Labs consisting of approximately 700+ web-enabled experiments which are designed for remote-operation. It provides remote-access to Labs in various disciplines of Science and Engineering. These Virtual Labs caters to students at the undergraduate level, post graduate level as well as to research scholars.
- e-ShodhSindhu (https://ess.inflibnet.ac.in/) is a collection of e-journals, e-journal archives and e-books on long-term access basis. It has 10,000+ e-journals, 31,35,000+ e-books. It provides access to qualitative electronic resources including full-text, bibliographic and factual databases to academic institutions at a lower rate of subscription.
- Shodhganga (https://shodhganga.inflibnet.ac.in/) is a platform for research students to deposit their Ph.D. theses and make it available to the entire scholarly community in open access. The repository has the ability to capture,

index, store, disseminate and preserve Electronic Theses and Dissertations submitted by the researchers.

- VIDWAN (https://vidwan.inflibnet.ac.in/) is a premier database and national research network which has profiles of scientists/researchers and other faculty members working at leading academic institutions and other Research & Development organisations in India.
- National Educational Alliance for Technology (NEAT)(https://neat.aicte-india.org/) is an initiative for skilling of learners in latest technologies through a Public-Private partnership model between the Government (through its implementing agency AICTE) and the Education Technology companies of India. It brings the best technological products in education pedagogy on a single platform for the convenience of learners.
- SAKSHAT (https://sakshat.ac.in/) is one Stop Education Portal for addressing all the education and learning related needs of students, scholars, teachers and lifelong learners. The portal provides the latest news, press releases, achievements etc. related to Ministry of HRD. So one can visit SAKSHAT to know the world of online learning.

Higher Education after COVID-19

In order to conduct classes, there is a centralised recommendations promoted by HEIs across the country

- Students count
- Faculty count
- Percentage of students via reservation
- Percentage of students with special needs
- Location
- Location COVID Status (Containment / Red / Amber / Green)

- Location type (Urban / Rural)

The new trends will allow the education sector to imagine new ways of teaching learning and some trends may be pointed as below:

- Learning may not be confined to classes or to any specific boundaries. Students may be the virtual learners with one teacher leading dosens of students in the new age. The learning modules may be modified to suit different learning styles and the learning contents may come from different sources to meet the learners' aspirations and needs. Students may pursue their learning in the new paradigm as per their choice.
- Many parents may be reluctant to send back their children to schools/colleges suddenly after the end of lockdown. Some poor family parents who have lost their livelihood during the pandemic may not be able to afford the expenditure to send their children to institutions. This may lead to home education for another few months.
- Student safety and well-being issues are important deciding factors for students and their parents for movement to international institutions for higher study. New modes of social distancing will continue for quite some time and may affect on-campus face to face teaching learning. Many international universities have been closed and are delivering all educational activities online. Many international conferences in higher education have been cancelled or turned into a series of webinars. So, the national and international student movement may be diminished.
- All will maintain social distancing and avoid warm handshake, hug, personal greeting, and intimacy for a long time. Invisible restrictions may constraint the fun & joy of campus life. Sports, Gyms, tournaments may be in low gear

for a longer period resulting less physical activities of students.

- The need for social distancing may imply lesser students in each class. So, most of the educational institutions may work in different shifts per day which may put more pressure on the teaching and administrative staff of the institution to manage.
- Learners from low-income families and disadvantaged groups are the more likely to suffer as they may not afford high-speed internet connection and required technical gadgets for online learning. It will widen the gap between privileged and unprivileged learners creating inequality.
- More and more students will depend on technology and digital solutions for teaching learning, entertainment and connecting themselves with the outside world. Students will use internet technology to communicate virtually with their teachers and fellow learners through E-mail, WhatsApp, Videoconference, Instant message, webinar or any other tool.
- Artificial Intelligence (AI) may help teachers to deal with assessment, evaluation, preparing mark-sheets and monitoring the performance of each student easily. AI may use digital platform extensively to reduce burden of examiner in handling examination and evaluation systems. If these activities are made simpler, the academicians would be able to concentrate more on course development, qualitative teaching-learning and skill development.
- Covid-19 has forced the human society to maintain social distancing. It has created more challenges to continue teaching learning by maintaining social distancing. To meet these challenges there is more demand for ODL and online modes of education and the same trend may continue in future also.

- Blended learning combines both face to face and online learning modes. Covid-19 has accelerated adoption of digital technologies to deliver education and encouraged the educational institutions to move towards blended mode of learning. All teachers and students became more technology savvy. The traditional face to face mode with post Covid-19 technology mode will lead the education towards blended mode of teaching learning and it may transform the structure of the education system.
- In India, lots of students or their parents take education loans for higher education. If the employment market does not pick up, student debt crises may rise and create serious issue. Students may face increased stress, anxiety and depression due to their student loans.
- There is no recruitment in Govt. sector and fresh graduates fear withdrawal of their job offers from private sectors because of the pandemic Covid-19 (Pravat, 2020b). Many Indians might have returned home after losing their jobs overseas due to Covid-19. Hence, the fresh students who are likely to enter the job market shortly may face difficulty in getting suitable employment.

Remedies that can be afforded

The way to go forward to bridge gap of teaching and learning process as given below,

- Regulatory flexibility on conducting classes, gathering teachers and examinations oriented.
- Creating centralised academic content in order to engage the students with Online Program Management.
- Educators and learners should be trained to utilise online teaching learning process using technology. Policy should be adopted by Government/educational institutions to provide free internet and free digital gadgets to all learners in order to encourage online learning as a result of which

people would get engaged and remain safe during pandemic (Pravat, 2020c).

- Immediate measures are required to lessen the effects of the pandemic on job offers, internship programs, and research projects.
- Many online learning platforms offer multiple programmes on the same subjects with different levels of certifications, methodology and assessment parameters. So, the quality of programmes may differ across different online learning platforms. Therefore, establishment of quality assurance mechanisms and quality benchmark for online learning programmes must be developed and offered by HEIs in India keeping in view of rapid growth of the online learning platforms.
- WHO has recently pointed out that the Covid-19 may never be eradicated and people will have to live with it. "It is important to put this on the table: this virus may become just another endemic virus in our communities, and this virus may never go away. HIV has not gone away, but we have come to terms with the virus.
- Across the globe, Indian traditional knowledge is well known for its scientific innovations, values and benefits to develop sustainable technologies and medicines and this knowledge systems in different fields should be integrated with a present-day mainstream higher education system.

Conclusion

This study has outlined various impacts of Covid-19 on higher education in India. The recent pandemic created an opportunity for change in pedagogical approaches and introduction of virtual education in all levels of education. As we do not know how long the pandemic situation will continue, a gradual move towards the online/virtual education is the demand of the current crisis. UGC and MHRD have lunched many virtual platforms with online depositories, e-books and other online teaching/learning materials. Combination of the traditional technologies (radio, TV, landline phones) with mobile/web technologies to a single platform with all depositories would enhance better accessibility and flexibility to education. This would involve upgrading the service platform to enable it to meet the required volume of educational demands of students. All service providers need to be mobilised to provide proper access to the educational service platforms to the disadvantaged groups of population also. Virtual education is the most preferred mode of education at this time of crisis due to the outbreak of Covid-19. The post Covid-19 education seems to be an education with widely accepted online/virtual education which may perhaps be a parallel system of education. This paper has not covered any statistical analysis on impact of Covid-19 on higher education however further in-depth study with statistical research may also be undertaken.

References

http://jgu.edu.in/blog/2020/06/29/impact-of-covid-19-on-higher-education-challenges-opportunities/#:~:text=Schools%20and%20universities%20have%20been,and%20colleges%20are%20currently%20impacted.

https://en.wikipedia.org/wiki/COVID-19_pandemic_lockdown_in_India

https://medium.com/@daiictweb/post-covid-19-higher-education-in-india-an-interview-with-dr-ks-dasgupta-41c8217205d3

https://www.aicte-india.org/sites/default/files/COVID-19%20Response%20Toolkit.pdf

Pravat Ku Jena. "Online learning during lockdown period for Covid-19 in India." *International Journal of Multidisciplinary Educational Research.* 2020c; 9,5(8):82-92.

Sandhya Ramesh. What it means for Covid to never go away and become endemic- like HIV, malaria, measles, 2020. Retrieved on June 2, 2020 from https://theprint.in/health/what-it-means-for-covid-tonever-go-away-and-become-endemic-like-hiv-malariameasles/ 423217/

UGC notice (29 April, 2020). UGC Guidelines on Examinations and Academic Calendar in view of COVID-l9 Pandemic Retrieved on June 5, 2020. From ttps://www.ugc.ac.in/pdfnews/5369929_Letterregarding-UGC-Guidelines-on-Examinations-and-Academic-Calendar.pdf

Wikipedia. *Covid-19 Pandemic in India*. Retrieved on May 20, 2020 from ttps://en.wikipedia.org/wiki/COVID-19_pandemic_in_India

14

Learning Environment: Student Centred

P. N. Lakshmi Shanmugam

Introduction

Teaching-Learning process was initiated by our ancestors in India through the system called Gurukulam. Gurukulam way of learning is wherein students or disciples live with the guru in the same house. The Guru is empowered the responsibility of transforming and educating the students. Education in the Gurukulam is blended along with the lifestyle that is being adopted and established by the Guru. Education embedded into the students is through a mixture of stories, theories and practicals, was done in a comprehensive way of learning and teaching, wherein students leaves the Gurukulam after completing the learning process to the satisfaction of the Guru. This ancient Gurukulam style of learning was the first teaching and learning process that got transformed into different ways. We Indians are proud to be the one who initiated this Gurukulam style of leaning that is being renamed as residential schools / Colleges. This Gurukulam learning slowly transformed into different ways as years passed.

Classroom based learning got evolved as the number of students joining into learning started increasing in an exponential manner. Classroom based learning involves face to face interaction among students and teachers. A teacher delivers the lecture by talking and explaining on the blackboard with a chalk. Students in classroom learning, actively participate in asking questions and getting their queries resolved. A lot of new teaching aids and techniques have emerged for example, overhead transparencies, power-point presentation etc. to take lectures and slowly transformed into whiteboard with markers, This transformation in technology slowly brought about a lot of advancement in teaching pedagogy.

Introduction of computers brought about the usage of LCD projectors in the lecture series. This totally transformed the teaching process by ways of preparation that a teacher does before taking the classes. The introduction of the internet into classroom through LCD presentation provides students with more opportunities to blend many learning materials from any part of the world. Video recordings by teacher was initially started as process by wherein the students were able to learn repeatedly. It was stored and reused through many storage devices which changed in accordance to the advancement of technology like CD, DVD and Pendrives. The advancement in internet brought about transformation in the reaching of live classes to the students in different locations at their own pace, breaking of the walls and boundary of classrooms.

The introduction of digital learning methods vary from using mobile devices to using extravagant software tools. Digital pedagogy is the learning and usage of modern digital technologies in teaching and learning. It is an attempt to change teaching and learning in a variety of ways through the thoughtful use of technology. It changes our way of life, ways of communication, way of thinking, feelings, channels of influence on other people, social skills and social behaviour.

Teachers will be able to prepare the learning materials using images, audio, video and animation and helps every student learn at their own pace and place, guide, help, plan future studies. Also, peer pressure will encourage students to attain their goals. With online assessments, teachers can develop a strategy based on the students' needs. The chance to adapt learning patterns for each student will close the learning gaps. They noted that personalised, appropriate and contextualised learning can increasingly be tailored based on the learner's own passions, strengths, needs, family, culture, and community. The opportunity to customise learning sequences for each student will make education more productive. Digital learning extends learning opportunities worldwide. It is remarkable that thousands of university courses by the best professors are available for free to anyone with a broadband connection. The shift to digital can boost student by game-based learning. Learning management system make it easy for teachers to create and manage groups of students. The teacher assesses their students online and track their progress through content based assessment and assignment.

Free and open content in digital platforms will be utilised by millions of the students like OER commons, e-textbooks, videos in online libraries. SWAYAM is a programme intitiated by Government of India and designed to achieve the three cardinal principles of Education Policy vis... access, equity and quality. This is done through a platform that facilitates hosting of all the courses, taught in classrooms from Class 9 till post-graduation to be accessed by anyone, anywhere at any time. All the courses are interactive, prepared by the best teachers in the country and are available, free of cost to any learner. It is user friendly and offers maximum flexibility to the users. It promotes high level of interaction and activity. Massive open online courses are free online courses available for anyone to enrol. It provides an affordable and flexible way to learn new skills, advance your career and deliver quality educational experiences at scale. Millions of people around the worlds use MOOCs for their career development, changing careers and lifelong learning. National Digital Library of India (NDLI) is a virtual repository of learning resources is sponsored and mentored by Ministry of Education, Government of India, through its National Mission on Education through Information and Communication Technology (NMEICT).

Conclusion

In this digital pedagogy the teacher's role is greater than the traditional role. They prepare E-content in text, audio or video form. Teachers can do anything within a course including enrol users, to assign a specific course to teacher, adding or changing e-content, activities and grading students. Teacher prepares gradebooks for monitoring attendance and assignment, results as well as keeping other information for each student. Teacher provides opportunities for class projects, discussion boards, and a built-in web-conferencing tool to the students. It provides unlimited access to learning content anytime and anywhere.

References

Abdullah, Melissa Ng Lee Yen (2016). "Interaction Effects of Gender and Motivational Beliefs on Self-Regulated Learning: A Study at ICT-Integrated Schools." *Malaysian Journal of Learning and Instruction*, 13 (1), 25-41. Retrieved from http://mjli.uum.edu.my/

Anupama Bhargava & Pathy, M.K., (2014) "Attitude of Student Teachers Towards Teaching Profession." *Turkish Online Journal of Distance Education*, 15(3), 27-36. Retrieved from http://tojde.anadolu.edu.tr /yonetin/icerik/makaleler/ 981-published.pdf

Arulsamy, (2009). *Application of ICT in Education.* New Delhi: Neelkamal Publication Pvt. Ltd.

Deepak Tiwari, (2006). *Methods of Teaching Computer.* New Delhi: Crescent Publishing Corporation.

Devendiran, G., Vakkil, M (2017) "Effectiveness of E-Content Package on Teaching IUPAC Nomenclature of Organic Chemistry at Undergraduate Level." *Journal of Educational Technology*, 14 (3), 49-54. Retrieved from http://www.imanagerpublications.com

Gage, N.L, (1964). "A Method for Improving Teacher Behavior." *Journal of Teacher Education.* NewDelhi: Shipra Publications.

Ismaic Thamarasseri, (2011). *Current Developments in Indian Education,* New Delhi: Kanishka Publishers.

John D. Ross, (2007). *Teaching and Learning Science.* United States of America: Wads Worth the Engage Learning.

Katherine S. Cennamo. John D.Ross.Peggy A-Ertmer, (2010). *Technology integration for meaningful classroom use.* United States of America: Wads Worth the Engage Learning.

Lalita Sinha, (2012), *Modern Trends in Teacher Education.* New Delhi: Ankit Publishing House.

Manoj Kumar Dash, (2010). *ICT in Teacher Development.* Hyderabad: Neelkamal Publications Pvt. Ltd.

Nishantroy, (2012), *Educational Technology.* New Delhi: Sonali Publications.

Rosenberg.M.J, (2001). *E-Learning strategies for delivering knowledge in the digital age.* New York: Tata MC Graw Hill. Pvt Ltd.

15

The Transitions and the Aporias: The Spectrum of Higher Education amid the Horror of Pandemic

Poulomi Modak

> Do not go gentle into that good night,
> Old age should burn and rave at close of day;
> Rage, rage against the dying of the light.
>
> (Thomas 1959)

Introduction: We Are All in This Together

British poet Dylan Thomas in his celebratory poem "Do not go gentle into that good night" urged his dying father not to go "gentle into that good night [death]" (1959; improvisation mine) instead "rage rage against the dying of the light" (ibid.). Since then the poem has been an encouraging piece of documentation to many to fight against whatever ceases them to live. Amidst these dark hours, Thomas's optimism can be a token of inspiration to not surrender easily to the unprecedented destructions aggravated by the horror of global pandemic. The economic disaster along with shattering of health system in almost every country and especially in this country during the pandemic crisis emerge greater concerns for one and all. In this grave circumstances the education system in school as well as in higher institutions encounter challenges without any prior precaution. While the school education has been affected mostly with the anticipation of increasing dropouts, the higher education has its own challenges to face and fight. United Nations in its

"Executive Summary" has mentioned that COVID-19 has "created the largest disruption of education systems in history" (2020, p. 2) affecting 1.6 billion learners worldwide (2020, p. 2). As human development cannot be blocked, though reduced for the time being, great minds and efficient thinkers have been making plans and creating new technologies to face the pandemic in present scenario and to prepare for the upcoming days. Needless to say, the far stretching aftermaths of the pandemic is simultaneously the biggest concern for the social thinkers and policy makers.

The outbreak of COVID-19 in India with its first detected case in January was followed by the extensive nationwide lockdown since March 25, 2020 to June and then the Unlock phases. Till this time the educational institutions are not permitted with any relaxations to restart the formal educational activities. Of course, the intention is appreciable that the government has put the health of the students at the foremost than the education. This worldwide closure has impacted profoundly the world's as well as the nation's student population. The closure of education institutions had its severe impact in many countries, as United Nations has mentioned: "Closures of educational institutions hamper the provision of essential services to children and communities, including access to nutritious food, affect the ability of many parents to work, and increase risks of violence against women and girls" (2020, p. 2). In India about 32 crore learner have been forced to be immobile due to the nation wide spread of the pandemic. However, the Higher Education Institutions have positively reacted to the biggest calamity of this century. On the contrary the crisis has stimulated innovative approaches in the field of education. What was previously sought as impossible to achieve, this sudden adversity in the education system ignites a colossal of motivation towards the desired and inevitable changes in the arena of teaching-learning paradigms.

Vistas of new world have already been enlightened with the advent of new perspectives, brilliant techniques, fresh outlooks, and moreover the everlasting patience of the efficient teachers who not only face the crises bravely but accept the new technologies in continuing the teaching-learning process. Students' engagement and enthusiasm in this entire period had surely been remarkable. While technology is moulding itself as the biggest source for providing information just a mouse-click or touch panel away, the role of the teacher or the educator in catering knowledge must undergo tremendous changes. It is an evident that majority of the teachers as well as the learners of this high-tech generation face tremendous confrontations in accessing the technologies smoothly as mostly this is their first-time experience in online mode of education. In order to analyse the nearly irrecoverable impacts of COVID-19 in higher education and consequently to evaluate the possible solutions to this catastrophe, the UNESCO sponsored International Institute for Higher Education in Latin America and the Caribbean (IESALC) has circulated a report "COVID-19 and higher education: Today and tomorrow" on 9 April 2020 regarding the "impact analysis, policy responses and recommendations" (UNESCO, 2020a, p. 1). The report has highlighted the irreducible challenges for the teachers:

> "Teachers are also impacted significantly at the workplace and professionally. First, the fact that not all HEIs [Higher Education Institutions] have strategies for the teaching continuity activity must be taken into account, and in this instance, temporary contracts may be terminated. Also, the most evident impact on teachers is the expectation, if not the demand, of the continuity of teaching activity using a virtual modality." (2020a, p. 6; improvisation mine)

Technology as an Elixir

The adaptation of technology is never easy but it is inevitable; it is the elixir in this morbid circumstance of global pandemic. The unavoidable discontinuity in "face-to-face activities of HEIs should be seen as an opportunity to rethink and, to the extent possible, redesign the teaching and learning processes" (UNESCO, 2020a, p. 8). In a world when everything is digitalised the knowledge about and accessibility to new technological avenues should be incorporated as essentials in modern teaching-learning paradigms.

In this COVID-19 scenario the galore of technological development has enormous significance in running the educational agenda if not satisfactorily but ceaselessly. The directives of Ministry of Human Research Development (MHRD) and University Grants Commission (UGC) to utilise the virtual platforms for the teach-learning process became imperative as soon as the nationwide lockdown began. Ministry of Human Resource Development (MHRD) has initiated numerous online courses through Study Webs of Active-Learning for Young Aspiring Minds or SWAYAM and other digital platforms. E-library and e-books have been of tremendous help in this challenged situation when purchasing books or physically visiting the libraries are nearly impossible. The technological tools that have been used by faculty during lockdown for teaching and learning through online modes and will definitely be used in coming times are Soom, Google Meets and Google Classrooms, Telegram, Skype Meet Up, Whatsapp, YouTube, etcetera. It is certainly challenging to embrace so abruptly the new phenomena of virtual teaching-learning modules. Of course, prior to COVID-19 breakout the online mode had already been a method of catering and engulfing knowledge through various platforms. However, the total seclusion from the external physical world has broadened the purview for internal revelation – for learning something new; for accepting the challenges so far unimagined about.

The webinar on "The Futures of Education after COVID-19: Regional Dialogue" organised by UNESCO on 16 June 2020 probes into the aftermath of COVID-19 in implementing education amongst the learners of all age. The "Synthesis Report" of the webinar summarises the positive as well as the negative impacts of this deadlock in coming times. Among the positive sides of this new phenomenon of education system the followings have been highlighted in the webinar: there will be an increased acceptability of online distance learning systems; the continuous development in the innovative models for higher education will prepare the students for creative work spaces and motivate them for research works and entrepreneurship (2020b, p. 5-6). On the contrary, the negative influences are much more concerning: the uneven distribution of resources in national and international levels will expand the divisions in empowering the teachers and learners; the constant decreasing in academic attainment will inevitably affect the students in future times (6). However, this deadlock can be converted into an opportunity for re-visioning the age old traditional methods of teaching learning processes to introduce advanced methods and new spaces. The pandemic has intrigued us to ponder over that the present "digital platforms [are] for distant and life-long learning" (UNESCO, 2020, p. 14; improvisation mine).

The Aporias and the Discrepancies

The paradigm shift in teaching-learning experiences is imminent during the pandemic havoc and unavoidable even after the end of this global catastrophe. The education systems worldwide were "swift to react and adapt" (United Nations, 2020, p. 12) the massive transformations in the process of catering knowledge and acquiring the same. But this is not a denial of the fact that the unequal distribution of learning modalities due to the socio-economic challenges has created a "digital divide" (United Nations, 2020, p. 24) amongst the learners which will continue to persist in the longer period of time as well. The far stretched demarcations in socio-economic backgrounds has its potential credibility in rising the aporias in educational inequality as it is likely possible for the learners from the higher socio-economic background to have better access to the digital devices or high-speed internet connections, compared to the learners belonging to the lower socio-economic background. In India the unfortunate deaths of the young children, after finding themselves incapable of affording digital platforms of expensive android mobiles or seamless internet connectivity, shock the nation to the core of its integrity. Developing countries like India face a lot of much more complicated issues to deal with this emergency. Not only fighting against the poor health infrastructure, the nation is still struggling in providing the basic amenities to its netisens. Thus, the digital space should be institutionalised in order to procure equal and inclusive scope of learning experiences to all.

This is specifically recommended by the United Nations to avoid the "digital divide" (2020, p. 24) and dropouts as much as possible.

It is a context of great concern that most of the Higher Education Institutions in India and in the developing world are not well equipped to materialise the educational technologies which have been well utilised in other parts of the world (Asees, 2020, para. 4). The worldwide emergency has widened up this discrepancies in the already existing education system by shrinking the possibilities for the forcibly displaced children, women, refugees, economically vulnerable children, students who are differently abled. The discontinuity in formal education system will surely contribute to influence human lives expanding beyond the horison of education only. Therefore, anticipatory measures are to be undertaken against the impending nutrition crisis for the young children, violence against the women and girls, and the unemployment for the grownups. Thus, "we need to ensure that education systems are more flexible, equitable, and inclusive" (United Nations, 2020, p. 23). The risk which may sustain in post-COVID-19 scenario is that the exclusion rate can form the "downward spiral" (United Nations, 2020, p. 26) statistics with the incessant exclusion of learners. It is important to rely on the digital modules for the time being but it is also important to not forget about the students who have minimum share in technological access. In such cases "Low-tech and no-tech approaches" (United Nations, 2020, p. 24) are essential to follow.

Maximisation of the Resources

Of course, the ideal approach of earning knowledge is through the human interaction in a space that is occupied physically by the teacher and the learner. Though the multifarious processes to re-establish the normalcy of the order of the world are on its progress through innovative experiments and new-age researches, the electronic medium can never imitate the true essence of a classroom or any form of space where people interact through human connection. The digital space can be useful in different ways but the 'digital divide' in countries like us is a bare truth. Then the question arises that how to confront the situation? In order to distribute the existing facilities to the largest possible section of the society, the resource maximisation is the prior motivated aspect in this regard. The following points can be taken into consideration for an equal distribution of the existing resources to the maximum learners:

- The need to promote Inclusive Learning
- Facilitating the E-libraries nationwide
- An opportunity to resurrect the All India Radio Stations in promoting education
- Free and open access to the archives of national libraries, archaeological departments
- Digitalisation of all the existing invaluable manuscripts in post-COVID-19 era
- Removal of technological barriers from the government's end by investing in the development of digital infrastructure and simultaneously lessening down the cost of connectivity charges
- Use of educational broadcasting to support the learners from remote areas

In addition to the aforementioned points it is equally important to conduct workshops and training programmes to entitle the teachers in fighting with this unusual crisis; as well as the teachers should be motivated in incorporating the advanced methods. Further, the sympathetic and supportive concerns should be laid out towards the parents who already are striving hard against the financial, mental, and mostly health hasards in order to merge with the changes in their children's education

Conclusion: Futuristic Approach(es)

It is certainly "too early to estimate the future profile of the higher education" (UNESCO, 2020a, p. 7) as the struggle is still persistent. However, the question which remains relevant till date is that once the world is healed with its old vigour and lively colour can we expect the virtual teaching-learning experience to call for an intermission for the sake of continuity of the age old tradition of classroom teaching? This question seems inappropriate as the evolution doctrines have always been instructive in adopting new discourses; facing challenges in order to survive in this world. It can be imagined that the process of virtual mode of education will remain effective in expanding its periphery even after the world recovers from this fatal disease. Certainly the new imaginations will continue in forming the educational policies in higher education in future times as well. "Smart Education" (UNESCO, 2020b, p. 7) is to be identified as an integral "strategic choice" in the new curriculum. Ramamoorthy in the article "Teaching in the Time of COVID" published in *The Hindu* on June 06 2020 rightfully observed that there should be new "equilibrium and a new normal for learning amid the present challenges" (para. 9). It is, therefore, not an exaggeration to conclude that the nation's negotiations with the 'new normal' will remain in motion to direct the higher education for the indefinite period of time.

References

Asees, Abdul. (2020). "Higher Education During COVID and Thereafter: Considerations for India and the Developing World." *Social Science Space.* Retrieved from https://www.socialsciencespace. com/ 2020/05/higher-education-during-covid-and-thereafter-considerations-for-india-and-the-developing-world.

Ramamoorthy, Saraswati. (2020, June 6). "Teaching in the Time of COVID". *The Hindu.* Retrieved fromhttps://www.thehindu. com/education/teaching-in-the-time-of-covid 19/article31766432.ece\.

Thomas, Dylan. (1959.) *Collected Poems: 1934-1953*, London: J. M. Dent & Sons Ltd.

UNESCO. (2020a, April 9). *COVID-19 and higher education: Today and tomorrow.* Retrieved fromhttp://www.iesalc.unesco.org/en/wp-content/uploads/2020/04/COVID-19-EN-090420-2.pdf.. (2020b, June 16). *The Futures of Education after COVID-19: Regional Dialogue.*

https://en.unesco.org/sites/default/files/synthesis_report_future_of_educ ation_webnair_1.pdf.

United Nations. (2020, August). *Policy Brief: Education during COVID 19 and beyond.* Retrieved from https://www.un.org/development /desa/ dspd/wpcontent/uploads/sites/22/2020/08/sg_policy_brief_covid-19_and_education_august_2020.pdf.

16

Digital Education to Strengthen the Learning Gaps during New Normal Situation in India

Prasanta Kumar Barik

Introduction

The new normal situation during COVID-19 propelled the use of contactless digital technology across India. Indian used the COVID-19 opportunity to further spread the use of digital technology. An important role was played by Digital India Vision of the Government of India which seems to be an instrument in solving the situation in the present scenario, where every sector is caught in a crisis because of COVID-19. All the sectors including business activities have been put to halt. It has badly affected the education sector too. Educational institutions are shut down and as a result, it is putting a lot of stress on students and youths for their education, admission to career-making courses, skill enhancement, employment opportunities, etc. As, per UNESCO, it has been observed that approximately 157 crore students across the globe are facing a do-or-die situation in terms of education.

This new normal situation during COVID-19 has forced us to re-plan and re-organise our education system within these five to six months. Every one of us is realising that the education system needs to change. Now the policymakers and the educationists need to think seriously about its systematic change. This new normal situation has allowed adopting digital technology in education. It has changed the system of education from teacher-centric to pupil centric. The face to face system of imparting education is being replaced with virtual mode by giving more flexibility to both teachers and the taught. It helped the teachers to work from home and allowed to provide education by the best teachers or resource persons in the world. Now, the boundary of the classroom has been extended far. Virtual learning again engages teachers and pupils with their books, contents, and syllabi but on different platforms. As a result, teachers and the pupils return to transact curriculum in a different track. Looking at these, challenges both the States & Central Government with the help of various government agencies have taken important initiatives to bring education on the right track. The role of government agencies like the Ministry of Education, Government of India, NCERT, NIEPA, SCERTS, AICTEs to provide benefits to the students or the young and energetic minds of the nation. In the present context, digital technology in education has a significant effect on pedagogy. Emerging technologies like online courses, e-learning technology, social networking sites, etc. are gradually being popular among learners. There is a variety of digital initiatives available for making pedagogical designs and planning instructional practice for excellent educational experiences. Here we will discuss some digital initiatives which are important for the learners basically during this new normal situation.

Swayam Prabha

Swayam Prabha is consists of 34 DTH educational channels. It provides a Standard educational program using the GSAT-15 Satellite for 24 hours. Everyday new content on different subjects for each class for at least four hours which would be repeated five more times in a day is telecasted. The contents are developed by National Programme on Technology Enhanced Learning (NPTEL), Indian Institute of Technologies (IITs), University Grants Commission (UGC), Consortium for Educational Communication (CEC), Indira Gandhi National Open University (IGNOU), National Council of Educational Research and Training (NCERT) and National NIOS. Web-portal of these channels is maintained by the INFLIBNET. Anyone can visit its website through *www.swayamprabha.gov.in.*

Swayam

Swayam is an online program initiated by the government of India and formed to attain the three basic principles of Educational Policy are access, equity, and quality. The objectives of this program are to provide the best teaching-learning resources to all, including the most disadvantaged. It seeks to bridge the digital divide for students who have until now remained untouched by the digital revolution and have not been able to join the mainstream of the knowledge economy. It offers courses for class 9th till post-graduation standards. SWAYAM facilities study material to the students enrolling from standard 9th to postgraduate level (PG) degree at one destination. The flexibility of this course is, it can be accessed by anyone, anywhere, and at any time. The courses are prepared by the top teachers in the nation to provide the study materials. These materials are available free of cost to the learners. Swayam has engaged more than a thousand topmost faculties and teachers from various disciplines who are associated with designing and developing courses and its content. Swayam is based on four quadrants formulas. They are (i) Video lecture, (ii) Reading materials that can be printed/downloaded (iii) self-assessment tests through tests and quisses, and (iv) an online discussion forum for clearing the doubts.

Shagun

SHAGUN is an online initiative develops by the Department of School Education, Government of India in collaboration with all 28 States and 8 Union Territories to provide online learning platforms for the teachers and the students. The term 'Shagun' is derived from two different words i.e. which indicates 'Shala', which means 'School' and 'Gunvatta' means 'Quality'. The combination of these two words indicates SHAGUN is a program which tries to bring quality in school education program by providing a suitable digital platform for interaction between the teacher and the students. There are three online learning initiatives which come under NREOR, DIKSHA, and e-Pathshala.

National Repository of Open Educational Resources (NROER)

NROER a digital initiative developed by the Ministry of Education, Government of India to share e-content among the teachers and the students. This platform helps to access e-libraries, e-books e-courses to its viewers. Here in this platform already 16000 registered users and 14527 e-learning resources are accessible. Students visiting the NROER platform are getting exposure to e-libraries, e-books, e-courses in different disciplines. This website can be accessed both in English and Hindi language by the viewers. Viewers are advised to enroll for the NROER and start learning lessons by themselves that are taught in the classroom. There is also a student assignment test provision under this portal. This platform facilitates learners with documents, interactive videos, audios, and images in different languages. It also provides a chance of self-paced -learning by each student. NROER is a cooperative platform of various institutions like SCERTs, SIERT, SIE, Vigyan Prasar, CCERT, Gujarat Institute of Educational Technology (GIET), and other stakeholders who are contributing to educational content. It was developed by CIET, NCERT New Delhi on 13th August 2013 during National Conference on ICT for School Education. NROER hosts a large number of educational resources in many subjects and different Indian languages for Primary, Secondary, and Senior Secondary classes. Available resources are in the form of videos, images, audios, documents, and interactive. NCERT books for all classes are available in flipbook format here too. All the contents available on NROER is under Creative Commons CC BY-SA 3.0 License.

Diksha

Digital Infrastructure for Knowledge Sharing (DIKSHA) serves as a unique initiative as National Digital Infrastructure for teachers across the nation. The purpose of this initiative is to build and maintain proper co-ordination of a teacher's life cycle from the time student teachers enroll in Teachers' Training Institutions to till they retire as teachers. Herewith this portal teacher's creativity and innovative ideas are identified at the national level. It also helps the teachers to learn and train themselves for which assessment resources will be available. It helps teachers to create training content, profile, in-class resources, assessment aids, news, and announcement and connect with the teacher community (https:// thekeralaeducation.blogspot.com). The Ministry of Education, Government of India has launched the National Digital Infrastructure for Teachers (DIKSHA) portal to equip teachers from 1st class to 12th class into the world of e-learning. The platform is available for both teachers and students requiring learning material. DIKSHA is one of a unique app that requires students and teachers to SCAN the QR code available in the book to access the prescribed learning material. With more than 80000 e-Books solely created to train and enhance the learning of Class 12th students, the aim of CBSE, NCERT, and States or Union Territories is to ensure that the students do not miss out on learning in case they miss out on physical classroom learning (https://www.jagranjosh.com/article s/list-of-digital-learning-platforms-for-the-students-by-mhrd-and-government-of-india-1584). The portal is available in multiple languages for students. Download the DIKSHA app from Google Play and iOS Store or use the website: diksha.gov.in to access the basic information on these initiatives.

e-Pathshala

This is an initiative jointly made by the Ministry of Education, Government of India, NCERT, and CIET in 2015. The main aim of establishing this portal is to disseminate e-resources like e-textbooks, videos, audios, periodicals, teacher training modules, and printed materials for the teachers, students, educators, parents, and researchers. This portal provides e-resources for Class-I to Class-XII standards including NCERT books. It is available in many Indian languages and the main intention behind the program is to ensure among the students that they should not miss any concept taught in the class. This digital repository provides opportunities for the students to access the e-resources in the best possible manner from home.

Nistha

National Initiatives for School Head's and Teachers Holistic Advancement is an integrated teacher training portal and mobile APP (Android) for capacity building of 42 lakhs elementary teachers. It is developed by the Department of school education and Literacy as a national mission to improve learning outcomes at the elementary level through an integrated teacher training program. It is a centrally sponsored scheme under Samagra Siksha. It is a capacity building program for improving the quality of school education through integrated teacher training. Nistha is the world's largest teacher's training program of its kind. The main aim of this initiative is to build competencies among all the teachers and school principals at the elementary level. This initiative is the first of its kind wherein standardised training modules are developed at the national level for all states and union territories. Through this program it focuses on competency and higher-order thinking skills-based teaching-learning; promotes experiential and joyful learning; trains all teachers and heads as first-level counselors; provides online monitoring and support system, and prepares activity-based training modules.

National Academic Depository (NAD)

National Academic Depository (NAD) is an initiative to provide an online storehouse to ensure easy access to and retrieval of an academic award by the user. It also validates and guarantees its authenticity and safe storage. The main intention is to make the digital empowerment of its citisens through this initiative. It is run by the University Grants Commission (UGC) that has tie-up with approximately 55 school boards, 359 state universities, 123 deemed universities, 47 central universities, and 260 private universities (https://www.jagranjosh.com/articles/list-of-digital-learning-platforms-for-the-students-by-mhrd-and-government-of-india-1584).

The Spoken Tutorial

It is free and open-source software for new users. Here the user can develop his or her own ability in different educational fields without the support of a physical teacher to improve employment potentials. It is self-learning and self-paced software. A new user can get e-resources in various subjects in more than 22 languages through this website.

National Digital Library

National Digital Library of India run by Ministry of Human Resource Development (MHRD) presently called as the Ministry of Education, Government of India under its National Mission on Education through Information and Communication Technology (NMEICT) to provide content to not just for school students but also students pursuing higher education and Ph.D. degree. In this portal more than three crore online resources are available. Also in this web portal, more than 50 lakh students have registered and have 20 lakh, active users. This facility can be accessed through the mobile app too. The NDL covers the content of all major domains of education.

Free and Open Source Software for Education (FOSSEE)

It is another important initiative that promotes the use of open-source software tools to improve the quality of education in the country. It is a project under NMEICT, Government of India. This project helps the students and the teachers to access freely available resources and download the e-resources without any cost. E-content materials such as spoken tutorials, interactive videos, audios, conferences, documentation on awareness programs, workshops, training, and internships, etc. are available freely. It also aims to reduce dependency on proprietary software in educational institutions (http://fossee.in).

Virtual Labs Project

Virtual Labs Project is another key initiative of the Government of India under the Department of Education and with the collaboration of the National Mission in Education through

Information Communication Technology (NMEICT). This portal helps for online classes and accessing e-resources through virtual labs. Now, it has already more than 2000 virtual experiments are uploaded for the students to study. This portal is developed by reputed 12 IITs in India establish virtual laboratories across the country.

E-Yantra

It is a portal providing effective and relevant education to all engineering and technical institutions on embeds systems and Robotics. Workshops are organised to impart students and the teachers on this platform. Here the users are provided with the facility to learn the basics of embedded systems and programming. This portal has helped more than 275 colleges across India to get the benefit (https://www.scholarify.in/digital-initiatives-higher-education)

Shodh Ganga

Under ShodhGanga portal, electronic Ph.D. theses and dissertations of different universities are deposited for open access by the research scholars and scholarly community. It is the reservoirs of Indian intellectual outputs to manage and maintain by the INFLIBNET center. At present more than 2, 85,851 text theses, 7873 synopses/pdfs/ fellowships have been uploaded by more than 463 Indian universities (https://www.sodhaganga.inflinnet.an.in).

Shodhgangotri

This is a platform where approved synopses in the electronic version are submitted to the universities for the registration of Ph.D. course by the research scholars. The main aim of this platform is to check the duplication in research work conducted by research scholars from different areas in different parts of India.

e-Shodh Sindhu

It is a platform where at present more than 15,000 national and international journals and books in electronic form are accessible.

This platform helps the educationists and scholars to access online educational resources in the best possible manner.

There are numerous initiatives and programs launched by the Government of India and the Ministry of Education for the young and talented aspirants. The digital world and e-learning are expanding its presence globally. Therefore, students, teachers, and learners are advised to make full use of these online resources, especially during the COVID-19 outbreak to avoid any obstacles in the path of learning.

References

Dutta. A., & Goswami, A.L. (2020). *Corona pandemic and higher education,* The Assam Tribune, p.4.

Dutta, A. (2020). "Impact of Digital Social Media on Indian higher education: Alternative approaches of online learning during Covid-19 pandemic crisis," *International Journals of Scientific and Research Publications,* Vol-10, Issue 5, May 2020.

Jena, P.K. (2020). "Online learning during lockdown period for covid-19 in India," *International Journal of Multidisciplinary in Educational Research,* Vol-9, Issue 5(8).

India Report Digital Education, June, 2020, *Department of School Education and Literacy,* Ministry of Human Resource Development, Government of India, New Delhi.

https://www.scholarify.in/digital-initiatives-higher-education/

https://ncert.nic.in/ict-initiatives

https://www.ugc.ac.in/pdfnews/9208605_Brochure-(National-Convention-on-Digital-Initiatives-for-Higher-Education).pdf

https://www.jagranjosh.com/articles/list-of-digital-learning-platforms-for-the-students-by-mhrd-and-government-of-india-1584

https://www.digitalindia.gov.in/

https://www.epw.in/engage/article/covid-19-and-digital-futures-india-prepared-build

https://www.ndtv.com/education/hrd-minister-launches-india-report-on-digital-education-during-covid-19

https://www.indiatoday.in/education-today/featurephilia/story/e-learning-boon-to-education-system-during-covid-19-lockdown-1670617-2020-04-24

17

Can Digital University Meet the Challenges of Higher Education?

Priyanka Bose (Das)

Introduction

Literacy in India is a key for socio-economic progress, and the Indian literacy rate is 74.04% (2011 census). Despite government programmes, India's literacy rate increased very slowly. There is a wide gender disparity in the literacy rate in India: effective literacy rates (age 7 and above) in 2011 were 82.14% for men and 65.46% for women. The low female literacy rate has a dramatically negative impact on family planning and population stabilisation efforts in India.

The rate varies throughout the world with developed nations having a rate of 99.2% (2013); Oceania having 71.3%; South and West Asia having 70.2% (2015) and sub-Saharan Africa at 64.0% (2015). Over 75% of the world's 781 million illiterate adults are found in South Asia, West Asia and sub-Saharan Africa and women represent almost two-thirds of all illiterate adults globally.

The institutional framework of higher education in India consists of Universities and Colleges. As reported in 2015, India has 760 universities and 38,498 colleges. There are three types of universities: Conventional Universities, Deemed Universities and Institutions of National Importance.

Higher education in India suffers from several systemic deficiencies. As a result, it continues to provide mounting number of unemployed graduates that are unemployable despite emerging shortages of skilled manpower in an increasing number of sectors. Higher education in India faces problems ranging from income and gender disparities in enrolment, to poor quality of faculty and teaching and even to a general lack of motivation and interest amongst students. On the whole, India has an enrolment rate of 9% which is similar to that of other lower middle income countries. The population that is enrolled in higher education consists largely of urban metropolitan dwellers. Rural enrolment in higher education is very low. There is also disparity of enrolment in higher education with respect to gender.

The few of the many reasons are –

1. Though fee regulatory agencies fix a fee that cover expenses incurred by an institution along with a basic surplus, many institutions have been charging a fee that makes the venture profit earing. This mushrooming institutes are much glamourous and less qualitative.

2. There is a huge gap between those who move out from school and who enroll in higher education system, which is really needed to be bridged. This gap occur due to –

    a. Long distance to be covered to reach the higher education institute.

    b. Expansive for many to get a car or hire it for going regularly to institute.

    c. Due to conservatism still prevailing in many areas and caste, religion the girls are deprived of higher education.

    d. Many have to earn money for family maintenance and specially girls have to take care of younger ones in family after completion of the school education. So they can't avail higher education at their own available time.

e. It is also difficult for physically challenged to attend the college regularly.

f. The special students (DIVYANGJAN) also feel difficult to cope with the requirement of higher education in the so called inclusive set up which is actually a theory even till now.

3. *Lacking a common platform:* In India, apart from UGC (University Grants Commission) there are several regulatory bodies like AICTE, MCI, BCI, NCTE and those under state governments. These individual bodies move in different paths, creating various hurdles like exams, teaching methods for students. So we need to bring all important regulatory bodies on a common platform and develop a common understanding and strategy for managing the change.

4. *Lacking sufficient faculty:* Shortage of quality faculty is proving to be a great stumbling block in the transformation of higher education in India. This has created a shortage of almost 54 percent in the faculty talent pool in higher education, such a deficiency will greatly prove to be a stumbling block.

5. *Lack of new teaching method:* The Indian higher education system has been following lecture and board method for several years. This has turned ineffective and insufficient in many areas. Besides, there is a lack of teacher's learning and development areas need which is should be in the form educating them. There are no approaches like mentoring, spot visits, practical educational tours and involvement in research projects with peers.

6. *Development of teachers:* Finally, there is no syllabus for integrating development concepts like emotional competencies, life skills and info-savvy skills. etc. Education institutions often lack the emphasis for pointing out on the learning outcomes than content teaching. Many

institutions never take the initiative to collaborate or participate with international institutes in order to get the exposure of digital learning methods or technologies.

7. *Accountability and performance of the teachers:* At present, there is no mechanism for ensuring the accountability and performance of professors in universities and colleges. This is unlike foreign universities where the performance of college faculty is evaluated by their peers and students.
8. *Problem with pedagogy:* Pedagogy and assessment are focused on input and rote learning; students have little opportunities to develop a wider range of transversal skills, including critical thinking, analytical reasoning, problem-solving and collaborative working.
9. *Infrastructural problem:* Inadequate infrastructure facility: in India many of the universities don't have adequate infrastructure or facilities to teach students. Even many private universities are running courses without classrooms. Internet and Wi-Fi facilities are still out of reach of many students.
10. *Lack of involvement of teachers in administrative issues:* Most of the professors and higher authorities do not like to take part in education related activities. They stick to their own growth and teaching only.
11. *Quota system:* Due to quota system the deserving candidates of general categories are ignored and on quota we have to select other person from reserved category though he is not suitable.

To cope with all these above mentioned difficulties of formal higher education system there emerged growing need for open and distance learning mode for higher education system.

The primary objective of the ODL is to provide knowledge and skills to those who did not have access to learning. The basic purpose of the open universities is to provide instruction to the learners at their doorsteps through various media and technology (UNESCO, 2002)

The concept of open learning and distance education system focuses on open access to education and training to make the learners free from the constraints of time and place, and offering flexible learning opportunities to individuals and groups of learners.

The advantage of technology in distance learning is that students can watch lectures before coming to class and engage in more interactive activities in the class

It also allows for a consistent delivery of content, because online videos can be pre-recorded and shared with the rest of the class online.

E-Learning has the possibility to support learning processes, collaboration, flexibility, and the distribution of education and training, as well as evaluation of content and skill in distance learning.

Previously, the open universities were more often used by young matriculated students who had not gained a study place at a "proper" university; but nowadays, students are more often adults in professional positions who want to enhance their qualifications, skills, and competences via e-learning by enrolling in web-based courses.

It is good for the elimination of face-to-face training and development costs both in monetary terms as well as in terms of productivity loss, as learners spend time away from their daily activities and jobs in order to participate in the face-to-face training sessions. e-Learning courses are available 24 X 7, location independent, and provide effective and efficient training means for learners in geographically dispersed areas and across time sones.

Some students may require digital literacies to participate successfully in everyday life increasingly mediated by technologies. To offer relevant learning experiences in distance learning, lecturers need to develop new skills and knowledge about technologies.

Students opting for Distance learning are able to care for their families and incorporate instruction on online courses and this can afford them the opportunity to work while they are raising their family and pursuing their full-time jobs. Distance learning can also benefits students because of flexibility about when and where they can engage in their learning ICTs can create opportunities for distance-learning institutions to provide distance-learning platforms, which can make it possible for many students situated far from the centers of learning to educate themselves.

Generally, it is believed that e-learning was designed for purposeful and disciplined students, because there is no direct contact with the lecturer, which may increase the demand for them to work independently. Distance learning in higher education can teach students skills and competencies of developing professional skills such as the skill of self-study, the ability to plan and organise, time management skills, the ability to solve problems, to take responsibility, to work under pressure, and to be creative and initiative.

Inspite of all the advantages, there are few challenges for open distance learning, like:

1. The high cost of information and communication infrastructure, and the dearth of technical expertise are another challenges in distance learning.
2. Sometimes the study material or open contents developed are difficult to follow, and as a result, reducing the enthusiasm of learners in their respective studies;
3. The lack of any clear quality assurance mechanism, which may result in unclear standards and by consequence, poor quality of distance education;
4. In distance-learning marginalised students, for example, the impaired and the economically disadvantaged ones may be further excluded from educational practices when ICT is used. Some students may not afford the use of technology if it is not free or subsidised. These students are also often

unable to use the ICT due to institutional failures to comply with legal and technical requirements for impaired students. There is a growing concern that distance learning is compromising the quality of education partly because one of the key challenges is lack of appropriate interaction practices

5. Language barrier is also a problem in distance education.
6. Another challenge for distance learning in higher education can be the problem of how the content of the course meets the expectations of students oriented on getting the opportunity of career growth, personal and professional development on the basis of distance learning.
7. problems caused by the lack of direct contact between student and lecturer;
8. problems associated with feeling of alienation and isolation from the student community;
9. problems associated with anxiety and concerns regarding the education process and learning results.

In my opinion we can solve few of the problems through a kind of Digital University which will assure us

1. The four pillars like – video lectures, e-content, discussion forum and self-assessment
2. Bachelor's or Master's degree without attending college or universities personally
3. Delivery of recorded lectures videography, question answer provision, query meet, online teacher student interaction and self-assessment e-content in the place of text book.
4. Overcomes the barrier of space, age bar, attendance, pace, scarcity of teachers, only Minimum qualification required to take admission in UG courses is 10+2 or equivalent from any UGC recognised Board/Council/Open School.

5. The most unique it is offering really a choice based credit system removing all boundaries and barriers of Science, Arts and Commerce.
6. Quality education and flawless examination system with unquestionable cost effective private guidance from experienced teachers to students whenever he requires.

The university will be unique in the sense that

1. Learning while earning has become a truth in this project. The employed students will be able to learn at their convenient time and achieve their academic goal while earning their livelihood.
2. Those who want to explore more and more subjects will be given ample scope for that in this Digital University.
3. High-tech technology including Power point presentation, slide show, video clippings are being used to provide uninterrupted classes to students.
4. It is totally virtual in the sense classes are live 24 X 7 hours and students will be able to follow each and every classes repeatedly and digitalised evaluation system. Students would be able to access the virtual libraries of different arena of the world through our web portal. References of the study materials can be downloaded as and when required.
5. Certificates/necessary documents would be delivered to the students through mail with security required.
6. As it is a cloud based classroom there is no barrier of in-take capacity which in case of most of the other universities students are deprived for this reason.
7. There is provision for self-assessment.
8. An all India based UGC recommended CBCS syllabus is offered for each subject and course which means the

students will really get an opportunity to choose their subject combination.

9. It does not have any stipulated time span within which a student has to complete the course which means the student will get ample freedom to learn according to their convenience.

10. A student who has passed in a certain number of semesters in UG/PG course from any University can continue pursuing subsequent semester from the Digital University, provided he/she brings the credit score, NOC and migration from the previous University.

11. Students' answer scripts will be stored in Computer memory. The students appearing for the term end examination will write their answer in electronic digi-pads provided in the scheduled examination centre.

12. Though it is virtual by Philosophy but it has every scope of teacher student quality interaction. Students may send their queries regarding delivered lectures or anything related to the topic anytime which will be conveyed to concerned teachers who will send their reply via e-mail to students.

13. It is democratic in nature as there is scope for students feedback on the lecture delivered by marking stars just beneath the video of the lecture. Again "Learners' engagement" will be monitored by tracking their participation in discussions and assignments.

14. The digital education is cost effective than traditional education as it provides a healthy support of renowned and experienced teachers from all over the world.

15. The WEB – CAMPUS is a mind blowing concept of this University where students will get ample freedom to share their thoughts on different burning issues, their academic problems in this Student BLOG.

16. This WEB-CAMPUS will help to develop leadership quality, motivation, we-feeling, a belongingness towards the University. Even it can be used for engaging students in area wise social activities under University Banner.

17. This university is the pioneer in WEB-based Student campus, where students get worldwide platform to share their views cultural activities which will be used for developing University Magasine.

References

Peter, Michael S. (1994). *Unlocking Open Learning, Centre for Distance Learning*, Monash University, Australia.

Prasad, V.S. (1992). "Dr. B.R. Ambedkar Open University: A Decennail Perspective", *Indian Journal of Open Learning*, Vol.1, No.2.

Reddy, L. (1995). *Consolidated Report of Counselling Feedback Reports of the year* 1993. Regional Services Division, IGNOU, New Delhi.

Rai, A. N. (2000). *Distance Education*, Authors Press.

Smith, P. and Mavis, K. (1989). Eds. *Distance Education and the mainstream,* Croon Helm. London.New York. Sydney.

Singh, B. et. al. (1993). *Correspondence or Distance Education in India: An In-depth Study Covering the Year* 1989-1990. Research Report, New Delhi: IGNOU.

Verma, A. (1999). *Learner Performance in Distance Education.* Commonwealth Publishers. New Delhi.

18

Mental Health of Students: Educational Implications, Issues and Challenges

Ritwika Laskar

Introduction

When a person says, "I have fever", we tend to get very careful. We advise them to go to the doctor or take some medicines. We tell them to take care of themselves. But, when somebody says, "I am not feeling good. I am not at peace and I don't know the reason behind my discomfort", we simply say "Oh! This is just a passing phase. Go for a movie or better still try some retail therapy." We very often fail to address this pertinent issue of mental health and at times perhaps unknowingly ignore it as something not so significant.

However, it is quite alarming that a considerable percentage of student population not only in India, but also in foreign countries are either diagnosed with some mental health issue or have been treated for the same. Not only students but also people successfully placed in life have reported the need for professional help due to psychological issues.

There can be an array of reasons that might impact the mental health of the students. Some of the common ones are –

- Childhood abuse, trauma, or neglect
- Social isolation or loneliness
- Experiencing discrimination and stigma

- Social disadvantage and / or poverty
- Bereavement (losing someone close to you)
- Severe or long-term stress
- Having a long-term physical health condition
- Drug and alcohol misuse
- Domestic violence or bullying
- Significant trauma as an adult, such as being involved in a serious incident in which one feared for one's life, or being the victim of a violent crime
- Physical causes – for example, a head injury or a neurological condition such as epilepsy can have an impact on one's behaviour and mood too.
- Hereditary

Mental Health, when defined broadly refers to a person's condition with regard to their psychological and emotional wellbeing. It plays a significant role in defining one's personality. It impacts the way we think, behave and conduct ourselves in our day-to-day lives.

A mentally healthy person can adapt himself or herself in any situation. Society has its taboos and prohibitions and for satisfactory social or personal living, the individual must learn to adapt to these. This presence of adaptability is one of the qualities of a mentally health person. A generally positive adjustment is indicative of good mental health. The ability to adjust and conform, to delimit one's behavior to the bounds of legality and respectability is certainly one facet of healthy personality.

Besides adaptability, optimism is another variable of mental health. Several studies have indicated that low achievers frequently expressed fear of failure in examination and lack of interest in studies, whereas high achievers were more optimistic about academic future and they aspired to achieve high standards.

Maladjusted students do less well in scholastic competition than do other students. Under achievers are more prone to feel helpless, rejected or isolated which would in turn affect their ability to adjust and adapt.

Student mental health issues are characterised as a student experiencing difficulties regulating their mood, thoughts or behavior. Looking at mental health from the educational point of view, mental health of the learner as well as of the teacher is of utmost importance for efficient learning and proper development of personality.

Importance of School

An infant spends majority of its time with the family. Gradually, however it is the school and the teachers who take over and assume an important place in ensuring a healthy climate for the benefit of the learners. The years of childhood and adolescence play a key factor in shaping young adults into who they will become and what their role in society will be. During these phases of life, children and teenagers spend a majority of their time in school, making this environment a crucial part of their life, well-being and development. From Kothari Commission (1964-66) to National Curriculum Framework (2010), issues relating to mental health and its subsequent role have been clearly articulated.

The school, as we all say is a miniature society. It can be said that children often learn to evaluate themselves in the world in which they live; from the opinion of their parents and teachers along with acceptability by peers. School environment plays an important role in the development of positive attitudes among students. It has to provide feelings of security among students along with a conducive environment for learning, which is free from fear, tension and frustration.

The co-curricular activities organised in schools also play a prominent role in channelising energy of the students in a positive and creative manner. Garfield, et al. (1969) specifically studied the relationship between creativity and mental health and came to the conclusion that there is a positive correlation between mental health and creativity. These activities help students in venting out their pent-up emotions.

The most alarming part of the entire discourse is that mental health difficulties in children and teenagers are often unrecognised. Consequently, young people commonly go without treatment which is known to be effective and this occurs at a crucial developmental stage when they should be laying the foundations for their personal, academic and economic advancements.

"The role that schools and teachers play in promoting positive mental health in children should not be underestimated. Creating a school ethos which promotes and builds strengths among students irrespective of their academic profile, can turn risk into resilience and significantly reduce the prevalence and impact of mental health disorders."

Good mental health is critical to children's success in school and life. Kellam (1975) in his study pointed out that the most important factors in mental health of the child is the degree to which the child masters basic educational tasks and earns approval of the classroom teachers. The implication of this claim clearly seem to be that a primary mental health function of schools is to ensure that all children master basic educational and social tasks and are given warm and personal recognition for doing so.

It is important to take into consideration some of the instances, which might otherwise appear trivial but do play a crucial role in manifesting disturbances among students encountering mental health issues:

- There is often a tendency to alienate that quiet little loner in the class, who never raises his/her hand, never answers any question asked and hardly smiles when the entire class goes on a roll after a joke is cracked. Instead of ruling the student out as an extraordinarily shy or uninterested individual, the teacher should rather try to get involved with him/her in a personal dialogue failing which the teacher might very well refer the student to the school counsellor.

- As teachers haven't we come across that stubborn lot whose naughtiness knows no bound? No matter how much we scold or warn them, nothing seems to work! Do we really consider the fact that perhaps they might be craving for attention? Do we really try to retrace our paths to the source points which might have induced these students to behave in a certain way that they have been doing?
- Also, what about that under achieving kid who has been really studying hard but turns nervous prior to the exam or the one who is damn intelligent but denies to write on the paper?

Here comes in the most important role of the teacher. It is important for them to identify such students and deal with them with compassion rather than rebuking them. A teacher should have the required knowledge about mental health.

Role of a Teacher

As teachers, we come across a plethora of diverse students who don't act the way they should be. Here comes the specific role of teachers and their need to deal with each student in a customised manner. The teacher plays a key role in ensuring positive mental health for the students besides identifying students who might be having mental health issues. Awareness of the teachers concerning behaviors associated with mental disorders is essential as they are in the unique position of observing student behavior on a daily basis. The first step is awareness, and the second step is bringing the concerns to the attention of the appropriate school staff who can provide assistance. The teacher plays a key role in ensuring positive mental health for the students. The teacher must have the knowledge of fundamental principles of human behavior to be able to tackle the problems of his/her students. The teacher also has to develop cooperation, team spirit and group participation among students. He/she should also try to develop a variety of interests in his/her students so that they are able to identify their potentials and engage themselves in co-curricular activities. Worthwhile activities of the students should be appreciated and encouraged. The teacher's behavior with the students should be of a friend, philosopher and guide. He/she plays an important role in making the students feel confident so that they are able to face all the challenges of life successfully.

When we talk about mental health of students, we have to keep in mind that the teacher's mental health also plays a pivotal role in the teaching-learning process. If the teacher does not have a sound mental health, then he or she cannot do justice to the job.

Conclusion

It is also important for teacher and student alike to understand that having a mental health issue does not make the person abnormal or different. Rather, these issues should be addressed in time and dealt with in a matured manner. Children with mental health issues should not be abandoned, rather they have to be treater with great care and affection. The society at large has to be accepting of these individuals.

References

Chauhan, S.S. (2013). *Advanced Educational Psychology* (7th Edition). New Delhi: Vikas Publishing House.

Chauhan, S.S. (2009). *Mental Hygiene – A Science of Adjustment* (2nd Edition). New Delhi: Allied Publishers.

Garfield, S.J., Cohen, H. A., and Roth, R. M. (1969). "Creativity and Mental Health." *The Journal of Educational Research*, 63 (4), 147-149

Kellam, S.G. (1975). "Mental Health and Going to School." *The Woodlawn Program of Assessment, Early Intervention, and Evaluation*. Chicago: University of Chicago Press.

19

A Shift towards Mobile Application and Online Education

Srabanti Mukhopadhyay

Introduction

Mobile technology is flourishing at a great pace in the education sector and has become a significant disruptive force in the field, especially during Corona crisis. The unprecedented situations due to Corona virus and thereby its preventive measures like lockdown has resulted in large scale disruptions in the life of the country and the individual. Most affected part of lockdown are education (especially teaching, learning, structure of schooling, assessment methodologies etc.) and small industries. At this time online learning and digital learning systems has come to rescue as alternative learning pathway and mobile application or mobile app as popular media for this. In this COVID-19 period mobile apps are using not only by the educators and educational institutions of India but also other countries (China, Austria, Egypt, Bhutan, Brasil etc.) of the world.

Online Education

Online education is electronically supported learning that relies on the internet for teacher/student interaction and the distribution of class materials (www.indiaeducation.net). Online education is a flexible instructional delivery system that encompasses any kind of learning that takes place via the internet (www.encyclopedia.com).

Mobile Application or Mobile App

The term 'App' is a short form of the term "Application software". An app is a self-contained program or piece of software designed to fulfil a particular purpose, an application, especially as downloaded by a user to a mobile device (Srilatha, 2017). According to Techopedia, a mobile application or an app, is a type of application software designed to run on a mobile device, such as a smartphone or tablet computer.

Mobile applications frequently serve to provide users with similar services to those accessed on PCs. Apps are generally small, individual software units with limited function. From the year 2002, apps are available through application distribution platform and are typically operated by the owner of the mobile operating system, like Google Play, Windows Phone Stores, Apple App Store, Amason, BlackBerry and others App World.

Educational app is a mobile application software that facilitates learning for students. These apps are making things easier for children to understand. There are many educational mobile apps like Khan Academy, Udemy, Duolingo, Reading Eggs, Mental UP, Kids Academy, Edmodo, Kahoot, SoloLearn, etc.

Review of Related Literature

Ling, C., Harnish, D. and Shehab, R. (2014) reported that when learning through examples with the mobile app, students performed better on problems that required them to apply their knowledge. Students in the app group felt strongly that mobile apps helped them understand the new concepts more clearly and were more confident in their ability to learn the new material more quickly than the control group.

Macaluso, K.D and Hughes, A (2016) made a study entitled 'The use of mobile apps to enhance student learning in introduction to Psychology'. They found that there was a significant increase in performance from pretest to post test for the app group on all measure. The app group answered more items correctly than the text group on the multiple choice and composite measures. There was no difference in the labelling measure and in self-reported ratings of enjoyableness between the app and the text conditions on the worksheet activity.

Ansari, M. D. and Tripathi, A. (2017) conducted a study on 'An investigation of effectiveness of mobile learning apps in higher education in India'. The objectives of the paper was to investigate the effectiveness of mobile learning apps in the higher education in India and to evaluates the role of mobile learning apps in students life. The study revealed that the role of mobile learning apps are increasing among students learning. It can be very useful in the higher education environment. The students had adequate knowledge and awareness to use mobile technology and the internet in their educational environment.

Pechenkina, E., Laurence, D. and Hunter, D. (2017) studied on using a gamified mobile app to increase student engagement, retention and academic achievement. The study investigated whether the use of a gamified mobile learning app influenced students' academic performance and boosted their engagement in the subject. They found that there was a positive correlation between students' scoring highly on the app and achieving higher academic grades.

From the review of different research studies it is clear that though the use of mobile apps for learning and its relationship with achievement or the effectiveness of it in higher education have been studied, but no work on the using pattern of mobile app and its use for online education during Corona crisis by the students was found. For this reason researcher chose to study the using pattern of mobile application, its use for online education by the students and problems of it during Corona crisis.

Objective

1. To study the using pattern of mobile app by the students

2. To find out the idea of the students regarding educational advantages of mobile app
3. To study the use of mobile app for online class during COVID-19 period
4. To study the problems faced by the students by using mobile app for online class

Methodology

The survey method was used for the conduct of the present study.

Population of the Study

The population of the study is comprised of the students studying at the undergraduate level of three colleges and three universities of Kolkata district (West Bengal).

Sample

In order to select the sample, the researcher has adopted Purposive Random Sampling technique. The present sample included 70 Honours students of different subjects from three colleges under the University of Calcutta and three universities of Kolkata district (West Bengal).

Tools

i. A personal information schedule was developed by the researcher to seek information regarding the background of the students. These include demographic variables like name of the student (optional), age, gender, caste, subject, stream and name of the college.

ii. A questionnaire has been prepared using Google form by the researcher which consists of 18 questions.

Validity of the Tools used

Content Validity was done by expert rating of items by 3 experts. Initially 19 items were taken. Those items which were rated as good and very good items were selected. For final selection of 18 items were taken. The interrater agreement model was used (Gregory, 2005) to see the reliability of the raters. The coefficient of content validity was 0.77.

Analysis

In order to interpret and analyse the data the researcher used both qualitative and quantitative analysis. Percentage calculation was used as the main technique for analysis of data. Narrative description was also done. Analysis was done for the study in two parts. In the first section it was the demographic information like age, caste, stream etc. In the second portion it was the using pattern of the mobile application in general and for online education during COVID-19 period and the problems of it among the students.

Major Findings

1. Most of the respondents (84.3%) were between 18 to 20 years old and remaining 15.7% were 21 to 23 years old. Majority (80%) of the samples were from General caste and only 10% of the samples were from Scheduled caste. Majority (85.7%) of the respondents were from Arts stream, 10% of them were from Science stream and remaining (4.3%) were from vocational stream.
2. Today education is not limited within the boundaries of classrooms. With the help of internet it has reached far and wide. One of the most useful technological approach in education of this century is Mobile App. Mobile Apps are very popular among the students. Majority (52.9%) of the students are using the mobile apps which are related with entertainment where as 23.5% students are using communication related mobile application.
3. This study has shown that most of the students are using more than one mobile application. 38.6% students of the sample are using 1 to 5 mobile apps where as 35.7% of the students are using 5 to 10 mobile apps. 20% respondents

are using 11 to 15 mobile apps for different purposes. Only 5.7% of the students are using 16 to 20 mobile applications for different reasons.

4. From the study it was found that students have more than one purpose to use mobile app. Most of the students (52.9%) use the mobile app for communication. The other purpose of mobile app usage are sharing documents with others (11.4%), access e-book, pdf etc. (10%) and accessing course information (7.1%).
5. Educational apps are making things easier for students to understand. Majority (55.1%) of the students are using educational app like BYJU'S, Duolingo, Edomo, Soom, Google meet, Google suit, Quis up, Kindle etc.
6. During the lockdown period, the education sector is affected by this closure. The educationists realised that we should change the way of the process of transmission of knowledge and methods of teaching. Most (58.6%) of the students think that mobile app is an alternative media for education during COVID-19 period. But 41.4% students of the study don't think so.
7. There are no time fixed time schedules when a student can access mobile application. Majority of the respondents (90%) think that mobile apps promote anytime and anywhere learning opportunities.
8. Mobile Application promotes anytime and anywhere learning opportunities due to different reasons as stated by the students of this study. Easy to access, easy to communicate with anyone, portability, flexibility, quicker access to information, easy to operate, huge platform and reaches out the whole globe etc. are the reasons as stated by the respondents of this study.
9. Online learning and teaching is the alternative learning pathway during Covid-19 period. It was noticed from the study that 78.6% of the students are attending the online

class during Carona crisis. But 21.4% of the students are not attending the online class due to various reasons.

10. Mobile apps helps the online learning and teaching. It was found from the study that the students are using different mobile application to attend the online class like Soom, Google meet, Skype, Teamlink, Edomo, Whatsapp, Microsoft teams etc.

11. Mobile application is helpful to improve parent-teacher communication. Teacher can attend quaries of the parents anytime and anywhere more quickly and efficiently through app like Classtree, Remind, Class Dojo etc. Most of the students (69.6%) believe that mobile apps are useful for parent teacher communication during COVID-19 period. They think that absence of face to face communication and to maintain the physical distance, it is only other medium in this period of distress. It links teacher and parents much more instantly. It creates transparency. Also, the parents can be constantly updated about the child's performance in class.

12. Mobile apps are best way for children to stay connected with their teachers and educators. 52.9% of the respondents think that mobile applications are useful to create direct connection between teacher and students. They express that this is possible for the facility of anytime anywhere communication. There is a possibility of clearance the doubts. But 47.1% of the students do not think so. They believe that nothing can replace physical presence.

13. Student can feel isolated during the online class through mobile app. 45.5 % of the sample has the feelings of isolation during the online class through mobile app. But 54.5% students of this study cannot feel isolated.

14. Students of this study are facing various problems by using mobile app for online class like absence of strong network,

poor signals, frequent disconnections, data usage, problems of attention, headache, problems of concentration etc.

15. Many teachers and students are not familiar with the technology. The big problem for online class through mobile app are the way of conducting or attending the class or integration of app with the lesson plan, issue of hacking, protection of personal information etc. Majority (85.1%) of the respondents believe that awareness regarding use of mobile app is required for online class.

Conclusion

Mobile technology especially mobile app has become essential need today. It creates a learning environment outside the framework of formal system. But at the same time it requires data pack. In this pandemic situation, teachers are trying to continue the teaching learning process through various apps. The results show active engagement of students with mobile apps for various reasons like communication, sharing documents, access e-book, pdf etc., and accessing course information. Majority of the respondents (90%) think that mobile apps promotes anytime and anywhere learning opportunities. Most of the students (78.6%) are attending the online class during Carona crisis. 45.5 % of the sample has the feelings of isolation during the online class through mobile app. Students of this study are facing various problems by using mobile app for online class like absence of strong network, poor signals, problems of attention and concentration, headache etc.

Mobile app is quite popular among the college students in India. From mobile app one can learn and share different things. It also provides opportunity for students to learn independently, to connect with teachers and instructors and enrich and expand their knowledge. We cannot ignore the potentiality of this. Mobile applications are now becoming as the most prominent way of interactive, systematic and smart learning as well as auto learning. This is the best way for students to stay connected with their education.

Limitations

1. The study was limited to three colleges and three universities of Kolkata.
2. The sample of the study was restricted to 70 female students only.
3. Only content validity was determined.

References

Ansari, M. D. and Tripathi, A. (2017). "An Investigation of Effectiveness of Mobile Learning Apps in Higher Education in India." *International Journal of Information Studies and Libraries*, 2(1), 33-40.

Gregory R. J. (2005). *Psychological testing – History, principle and application.* Delhi: Pearson (Education) Singapore Pvt. Ltd.

Ling, C., Harnish, D. and Shehab, R. (2014). *Educational Apps: Using Mobile Applications to enhance Student Learning of Statistical Concepts.* Retrieved September 12, 2020 from https://www.researchgate.net.

Macaluso, K. D. and Hughes, A. (2016). "The use of mobile apps to enhance student learning in introduction to Psychology." *Teaching of Psychology*, 43(1), 48-52.

Pechenkina, E., Laurence, D. and Hunter, D. (2017). *Using a gamified mobile app to increase student engagement, retention and academic achievement.* Retrieved September 15, 2020 from https://www.researchgate.net.

Srilatha, G. (2017). "Technology Applications in Education with special reference to Apps." *Edutracks*, 16 (7), 10-13.

20

Digital Divide in the 'New' Normal Education System: The Indian Scenario

Sumita Chatterjee

Introduction

The Global Emergency of Covid-19 pandemic confronts US All with Unpredictable Disruptive situations which have changed our daily lives, economics, political decisions and the educational system. The whole world is grinding to a halt. Advanced nations with most weapons, best brains and biggest banks are even struggling hard against an invisible enemy and yet 'learning' didn't stop. We have started adapting to a drastically changed education system that exists outside 'Classroom', 'Teacher' and 'Institution'. As the lockdown continues with no firm end in sight, 'Online learning' has been taken into consideration in order to keep the teaching-learning process on track. Impoverished socio-economic conditions, poor internet connectivity and inappropriate teaching techniques are among the many hindrances in the way of implementing e-learning, and hence, millions of students as well as teachers are getting deprived of such education. Teaching learning process is the heart of education. It is the most powerful instrument which brings about the desired changes in the students. NCF 2005 also highlights the value of interaction with the environment, nature, things, people, etc. – to enhance learning. School and classroom environment being an important part of interaction needs to be modified to a greater extent. The basic issue considered in this paper is concerned with technological threat in school environment. Modern era is blessed with advancement of technology. As the time passes with the technological advancement students are blessed with different gadgets. Multitasking with mobile phone is a very common phenomenon for a student. In a developing country, like India, where a major percentage of the population lies below the poverty line, we need to realise that our education system caters to students who belong to this BPL percentage. There are students who do not have a phone to communicate. Some who have the phone; they do not poses an android phone, to do a class on Soom or Access Google Scholar or Google classroom. And still there are many who poses the android but do not have the money to recharge Internet packages.

Now a day's mobile phone has suddenly replaced all the teaching tools of the World. The mobile phone exerts increasingly more influence on our everyday life. Internet based activities on mobile phones expand their reach beyond the economic and social field. Physically today's classroom is similar in layout and process to the classroom of 20 or even 50 years ago. Blackboard still dominates in a revised version of whiteboard. Despite many predictions since the 1950s television supplements lectures. Video cassettes recorder, compact disc recorder, network computers and computer software has brought some changes in class room settings but another digital technology are forcing to change the dominant paradigm of classroom based education. Today more than out of 6 people worldwide are using mobile phones (James Kats, 2009). A culture of perceptual contacts has come together with a loss of a sense of place and a potential for amusing ourselves to death: Students now easily communicate with the world beyond classrooms and are engaged with nearly endless entertainment and distractions.

Today, education is not just teacher centric, student centric but it is technology centric also. In today's competitive age the technology has evolved into facets of education that encompasses within "e-learning", computer and web based learning or training. At the same time the law of right of children to free and compulsory education at, 2009 which came force on 1st April, 2010, have raised the need of educators in every corner of the country. And the technology will play a vital role in bringing up the uniformity of information download.

A mobile phone in hand seems almost to contain some sort of energy all its own. It empowers the human being to go to new level of communication. This might commonly be seen as good for the students, but it has plenty of negative aspects. For instance, when student text messages each other they are given a chance to say things, they probably would never have said face to face. They do not have to immediately face their peers after pressing "send". They can say something harsh and biting without having to face the consequences directly. Students in school are inattentive in class, they miss out the lesson being taught, and the entire concentration goes upon to the mobile phone and not to the study. Random using of SMS directs the students to develop incorrect spellings. They have also tenacity to solve mathematical problem with the help of mobile calculator. The students have the tendency to avail the free night-talk time facility while studying late night, which in the next day results to the skipping of schools. Kubey, 2009 suggested that the heavy use of technology for recreational purpose for school students are highly correlated with reduced academic performance. Similarly Auckerman in 2008 found that 68% of the students received poor grade who used cell phone.

Concerned over the excessive use of mobile phone by the students, the Union government plans to conduct a study to find out its negative effects on health and academics. Indian Council of Medical Research (ICMR) has conducted a study which reveals that prolonged use of mobile phone can caused sleep-disorder, memory lapse and hearing impairment among the students. The Himachal government has banned the use of mobile phone on January 23rd in the year 2008 followed by the government of Kerala also banned it; under 16 children cannot use the mobile phone. Taking the first step forward the Federal Health Ministry of India ordered the first largest study on effect of radio frequency radiation (RFR) emitted from mobile phone. In India including Kolkata, the mobile fever has reached a high pitch, the latest version of mobile phones, with it's virtually add-on features is affecting the future generation regularly. So urgent awareness is needed regarding the discriminate use of mobile phone in relation with the academic achievement of secondary school students. As every month India adds another 1.5 mobile subscriber to the 28 million mobile phone users registered last December 2005, (source – Basu Tapati & Mukherjee Sujata,

The mobile mania in India: SMS revolution and MMS controversies) and most of them belong to the younger generation and school students.

The present study are to find out that what have led to the sudden mobile phone boom in India. Education as an instrument of social change should take up the responsibility to find out these answers, to save the technological threat for the new generation such that natural, purposive, harmonious development of all powers and faculties of human body may develop spontaneously.

Objectives of the Study

1. To compare the usage of mobile phones between boys and girls of secondary school.
2. To study the effect of mobile phone used by the secondary school students in terms of spelling error.
3. To compare the usage of mobile phone in rural and urban secondary schools.

Sample

Schools of Rural and Urban area

Tools for the Study

A 20 items questionnaire is developed for secondary school students to explore the usage of mobile phones in school.

Analysis

Table 1. Gender and Class Wise Break up of the Sample

Class	**Urban**		**Rural**	
	Boys	Girls	Boys	Girls
IX	25	25	25	25
X	25	25	25	25
Total	50	50	50	50
Sum total	**100**		**100**	

Table 2. Class Wise Break up of the user and Non-user of Mobile Phone by the School Students

	User	Non-user
Urban	100%	-
Rural	75%	25%
Total		

Table 3.1. Gender Wise usage of Mobile Phone Facilities. Boys

Class	Phone only	SMS only	Internet only	Games only
IX	41%	13%	22%	24%
X	44%	6%	24%	26%

Table 3.2. Gender Wise usage of Mobile Phone Facilities. Girls

Class	Phone only	SMS only	Internet only	Games only
IX	65%	8%	5%	22%
X	67%	4%	6%	23%

Table 5. Using of Mobile Phone – Gender wise

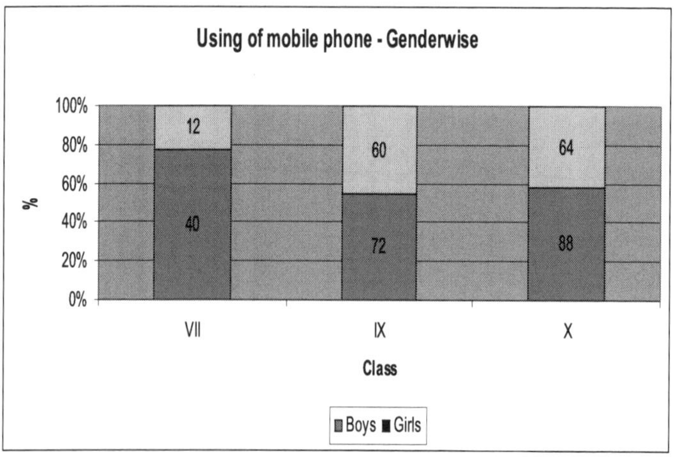

Findings

In case of first objective it has been found that most of the boys and girls know how to use mobile phones. Both boys and girls feel that it is a necessary item. On an average both girls and boys start using mobile phone from class IX. Girls use less mobile phone than boys. And they also prefer to call rather than text messaging. Both boys and girls play more games in mobile phone.

Incase of the second objective spelling error is prominent maximum in the rural schools but some students in the urban schools have also made spelling error. Due to short message service (SMS) the spelling error and grammatical error are much more pronounced and students have a tendency of mathematical calculations with the help of mobile calculator.

In case of third objective most of the boys and girls know how to use mobile phone irrespective of different classes. Although urban school students are more modern-phone friendly rather than rural school students. Urban school students use more modern-phone than the rural students. Regarding internet and game facilities urban students from secondary schools are more likely to use 3G phones with internet and new technology rather than rural students.

Conclusion and Discussion

The social networking sites (SNS) such as Face book, Twitter, My space have become an overnight phenomenon and are attracting young students by the millions resulting in inattentiveness and lower academic grades. Mobile phones have become an important accessory of high-school students since 1990. Although parents want to reach their children before and after school hours, but incidentally young students are distracted from their school work. Now a days internet, mobile phone, can be a very good source of education, as well as some specific usage of phone may harm the students in every field of life. Prolonged uses of mobile phones have a detrimental effect on teenagers' language and mathematics skill. Constant use of ear piece hampers the health of the students and also later on the study of the secondary school students also. Despite their convenience mobile phone can pose threat to school children physically, mentally and emotionally. The study shows that there is a need of modification of usage of mobile phone urgently. School students could be provided mobile phones with basic facilities only. Parents must be aware of the negative aspect of it. Modern era is blessed with different technological advancement, so these blessings should be taken qualitatively by the future citisens so that all round natural, normal, healthy development of personality of the school students may be taken into consideration.

Teachers are the greatest assets of any education system. A variety of teaching strategies are particularly appropriate for fostering sustainable living. The best hope for learning to live sustainably lies in schooling that is "Smart by nature". It includes experiencing the natural world. Teachers are in a prime position to be able to weave these basics throughout the curriculum at every grade level. The goal of education in this new age is to prepare students to use their skills to solve real world problem. So proper curriculum should be framed considering both natural assets and technological assets, so that children may interact both qualitatively and quantitatively. NCF has defined the term 'Curriculum Framework' as a plan that interprets educational aims vis-à-vis both individual and society to know the kind of learning experiences. The constructs of 'Environmental Education' and 'Education for Sustainability' are complex and contested issues. Hence there could be differences of opinions. Individual learner should have knowledge, values and skills to be active, technologically. He should be sound always but not neglecting the traditional student teacher interaction such that they may participate at the different levels within the society, locally and globally, to create a sustainable society.

References

Agarwal, D.D. *Educational Technology*. Book, (2004).

Haste, A *The role of mobile phones in young people's lives*. Croydon, UK: Nestle Trust. (2005).

Merry, P.Domlija & Mackensie N. *Global mobile forecasts to 2010* (5th Ed.). London: Information, Telecommunication & Media Inc. (2005).

Krishnamurthy, R.C. *Educational Technology: Expanding our vision.* Authors Press (2003).

Internet and American Family Life (PEW). (2005a). *A decade of adoption: How the internet has woven itself into American life.* <http://www.pewinternet.org/

pdfs/Internet_Status _2005.pdf/> Retrieved 05.03.

21

Signs of Teacher Burnout and Socio-Emotional Support during Covid-19

Sushant Kumar Nayak

Introduction

> "With school being held virtually as a result of the COVID-19 pandemic, teacher burnout is certainly still a key topic. It's easy to feel more isolated, alone, and anxious. Learning a whole new normal – whether it is adjusting to the new homework environment, the distance learning platform, or just monitoring the current pandemic crisis –can be overwhelming. As a result, stress that may have already been present is exacerbated,"
>
> Dr. Crestie Smith

It is important, as teachers, to maintain collegial contact through phone calls, audio and/or video conferencing, online classes and e-mails. Without a doubt, the teachers are going through the same things, feeling those same apprehensions and falling to burn out syndrome. That's why the support we can provide to one another is invaluable, just as it is during this unprecedented time till the normal school environment restored. Burn out is a work related syndrome that most often occurs in face to face service condition and constant interaction (Farber, 1991). It is a gap between expectations of successful professional performance and an observed far less satisfying reality. Burn out is a prolonged response to chronic emotional and interpersonal stressors on the job and is defined by the dimensions of exhaustion, cynicism and inefficiency (Maslach, Leiter, 2001).

Burn out has been associated with various forms of job withdrawal – absenteeism, intention to leave the job, indifferent attitude towards professional work, low professional commitment and actual turnover. However, for people who stay on the job; burn out leads to lower productivity and effectiveness in work. People who is experiencing burn out can have a negative impact on their colleagues, both by causing greater personal conflict and disrupting job tasks. Thus burnout can be contagious and perpetuate itself through informal interaction of the job. On the other hand burn out has a negative consequence for students as well (Burkee et. al, 1996) and for teacher families (Westman, 2001). The exhaustion component of burn out is more prone to health hasards and negative effects on mental health, anxiety, drops in self-esteem.

Objectives

In the tune of the nature of the problem, the researcher has formulated the following objectives for the present study. They are;

1. To highlight Potential sources of burnout among teachers.
2. To enlist Potential symptoms of teachers experiencing burnout.
3. To suggest the measures that compensates the teacher burnout during these covid-19 times with the help of socio emotional support.
4. To enlist various ways and methods to cope with the stress and teacher burnout

Background of the Study

In recent decades, Maslach's work on burnout has emerged as the dominant framework for studying burnout because of the defining psychological constructs she developed. Particularly, scholars have adopted the MBI (Maslach Burnout Inventory) scale developed by Maslach and Jackson (1981) which measures the psychological syndrome of burnout in three dimensions: emotional exhaustion, cynicism, and inefficacy.

Emotional Exhaustion

This is the core element of burnout and the most obvious manifestation of this complex syndrome. Maslach et al. (2001) noted that when people describe themselves or others as experiencing burnout, they most often refer to the experience of exhaustion. Evers et al. (2004) referred it as a draining source of emotion and enthusiasm for professional work. Schwarser et al. (2000) described fatigue, debilitation, loss of energy, and wearing out as characteristics of this component. However, emotional exhaustion is a personal psychological status which cannot capture other behaviours that relate to burnout. Maslach et al. argued that "*the emotional demands of the work can exhaust a service provider's capacity to be involved with, and responsive to, the needs of service recipients*" (p. 403).

Cynicism / depersonalisation

According to Maslach (1976), besides experiencing emotional exhaustion, human service providers or teachers who burn out tend to become more indifferent to the people they serve or to their colleagues. Maslach described this syndrome as cynicism or depersonalisation. This is a form of strong pessimistic attitude and low feeling within the working periphery, posing a threat to the cohesiveness of staffs and professional motivation of the group. Depersonalisation is to actively ignore the service recipients in an attempt to put distance between them and oneself (Maslach et al., 2001). Evers, et al. (2004) defines depersonalisation as "*a negative callous and detached attitude towards the people who one works with, i.e. patients, students*" (p. 132).

Exhaustion or depersonalisation might interfere with effectiveness. When a person feels exhausted or indifferent toward serving or helping people, it is difficult to gain a sense of accomplishment. According to Bandura (1997), self-efficacy reflects an individual's beliefs in his or her own capabilities to pursue a course of action to meet given situational demands. Therefore, a teacher who is inefficacious may have lower competence in his or her own capabilities in instructional activities. Maslach et al. (2001) suggested that "*the lack of efficacy seems to arise more clearly from a lack of relevant resources, whereas exhaustion and cynicism emerge from the presence of work overload and social conflict* (p. 403)."

Stressor

A stressor is any event, experience or environment stimulus that causes stress in an individual. These events or experiences are perceived as threats or challenges to the individual psychologically leading to negative outcomes in performance. Stress is defined by Seyle is *"a non-specific response of the body reacts to a physiological level to any type of demand"*. These demands are called *stressors*. We have the ability to perceive an event as pleasant or unpleasant and this perception plays an integral part in stressors development. The presence of stressor over an extended period of time can eventually deplete the person's physical, emotional and professional efficiency. The following warning signs of negative stress (Jerry, McBeath, 1990) are:

Emotional Sign:	Behavioural signs:	Physical signs:
– General Irritability – Boredom &Stagnation – Mind going blank – Desire to quit job – Unable to enjoy or compliment colleagues success – Free floating anxiety – Unknown fear – Always feeling under pressure – Disappointment with self and others – Feeling life is not much fun	– Tendency to overwork – Difficulty with routine daily work – Decrease in job performance – Less time for recreation – Forgetting deadlines, appointments – Blaming others for poor performance – Making a foolish mistakes – Automatic expression of negative feelings – Restlessness	– Fatigues – Headache – Weakness – Weight gain or loss – Insomnia – Stuttering or other speech difficulties – Vomiting – Trembling and nervous tics – Missed menstrual cycle

Previous researches in the field pointed out that once teacher burnout has been developed, it is easier to prevent it rather than to reverse it. If one recognise the warning signs of impending burnout in himself / herself, it will get worse if he/she leave it alone. But if one take steps to get one's life back into balance, one can prevent burnout from becoming a full-blown breakdown. Tims, Bakker and Derks (2013) showed that employees who craft their own job demands and resources increase their levels of work engagement and reduce the risk of burnout. Recent research suggests that employees with only mild symptoms of burnout use a range of strategies e.g. selection, optimisation, compensation (Bakker, Demerouti, and Leiter, 2014) to keep their job performance at acceptable levels. Besides studies related to factors leading to teacher burnout, studies related to its solutions and prevention strategies have also been conducted.

Method

Meta-analysis type study and qualitative description method has been adopted in this paper.

Expected Outcomes

Hendrickson (1979) discussed how to recognise teacher burnout and what to do about it. He offered seventeen suggestions for fighting burnout. Reed (1979) gave suggestions for preventing teacher burnout which include changing grade levels taught, building up self-esteem through positive reinforcement, involving teachers in decision making, promoting professional growth, releasing the pressure etc. A similar study was done by Sabel and Sabel (1982) describing burnout syndrome among special education teachers. They discussed burnout reducing techniques consisting of reduction of student-teacher ratio, shorter work hours, shared student load and training in stress management. Some techniques which can be used to prevent burnout problem are mention below:

- keeping a stable constructive relationship with colleagues and administrators;

- seeking assistance from professional counselors in case of occupational or personal distress;
- practicing a healthier lifestyle involving exercise, meditation, relaxation, and proper nutrition;
- acquiring proper time-management skills;
- accepting the personal and situational limitations and avoiding being overly perfectionist;
- striking a balance between professional time and personal time;
- setting realistic goals and priorities and scheduling accordingly

With this some other methods have been suggested to cope with teacher burnout with the help of Socio-Emotional Support is:

- Take care of your health
- Turning things around
- Trust students more
- Look for the positive
- Help another teacher
- Learn something new and share it with your students
    - ➢ Start the day with meditation: One should start the day spending at least fifteen minutes mediating or reading something inspiring.
    - ➢ *Develop healthy habits:* Development of healthy habits will provide energy to deal with life's hassles and demand.
    - ➢ *Management of time:* Proper management of time will help in eliminating stress.
    - ➢ *Have a break from technology:* Shut down all gadgets and relaxed your body and mind.

- *Avoid unnecessary stress:* Be positive and try to avoid unnecessary stress.
- *Be creative:* Thinking in creative manner will fill you with pleasure.
- *Have Realistic Goals:* Setting the goals high is motivating, but setting it too high can be stressful.
- *Avoid Conflicts:* Avoiding conflicts will save a lot of time and energy.
- *Believe in yourself:* Do not do others want. Take your own advice and do what you want.
- *Positive and optimistic attitude towards profession:* Positive thinking and optimistic attitude will make you free from stress.

Conclusion

The present article not only explained burnout among teachers but also explained how teachers can actively work to prevent burnout and also provided some techniques that faculty can take in order to heal from burnout and return to their previous state of health and pedagogical success during this Covid-19 crisis. Teachers should endeavor to attend stress-management interventions, not only for themselves but to understand others around them better. Intervention programs can be prepared in co-operation with administrators and counselors to prevent teachers burnout. Teachers with high levels of burnout need help in structurally changing their working conditions and health status, and we hope that the present article offers a framework with which this can be achieved.

References

Aseem, S.M., and Nasir, N.A., (2008), "A study of job burnout among university teachers", *Psychology & Developing Societies*, 20 (1), pp. 51-64.

Bakker, A. B., Demerouti, E., and Leiter, M. P. (2014). "Burnout and job performance: The moderating role of selection, optimisation, and compensation strate-gies." *Journal of Occupational Health Psychology, 19*, 96–107. http://dx.doi.org/10.1037/a0035062

Bartlett, L. (2004). "Expanding teacher work roles: A resource for retention or a recipe for overwork?" *Journal of Education Policy, 19*, 565-582.

Brock, B. L. and Grady, M. L. (2002). "Avoiding burnout: A principal's guide to keeping the fire alive." *Thousand Oaks, CA: Corwin Press.*

Cooper, C.L., and Cartwright, S., (1994), "Healthy mind, healthy organisation: A proactive approach to occupational stress", *Human Relations,* 47, pp. 455-470.

Daniels, K., and Guppy, A., (1992), *"Control, information-seeking preferences, occupational stressors and psychological well-being",* Work and Stress, 6, pp.347-353.

Freudenberger, H. J. (1974). "Staff burnout." *Journal of Social Issues, 30*, 159-165.

Gmelch, W. H., Wilke, P. K., and Lovrich, N. P., (1986), "Dimensions of stress among university faculty: Factor-analytic results from a national study", *Research in Higher Education,* 24, pp. 266-286.

Gupta Madhu & Rani Surekha (2014) "Burnout: a serious problem prevalent among teachers In the present times," *Bhartiyam international journal of education & research,* Volume 4, Issue 1, December 2014, pp.1-9.

Hendrickson, B. (1979). "Teacher burnout: How to recognise it; what to do about it." *Learning, 7*(5) 36-39.

Hogan, J. M., Carlson, J. G., and Dua, J., (2002), "Stressors and stress reactions among university personnel", *International Journal of Stress Management*, 9, pp. 289-310.

Kahn, R. (1986). "Job burnout: Prevention and remedies." *Educational Research Quarterly, 11*(1), 33.

Kaur, S., (2008), "Occupational stress in relation to teacher effectiveness among secondary school teachers", *EduTracks.*, 7 (10), June, pp. 27-29.

Kumar, N., (2007), *Influence of certain psycho-sociological factors on the occupational stress among the public and private school teachers of Orissa,* Ph.D. Thesis submitted to Utkal University.

Lieberman, A., and Miller, L. (1999). *Teachers transforming their world and their work.* Alexandria, VA: Association for Supervision and Curriculum Development. Pp. 104, New York, NY: Teachers College Press.

Lowenstein, L.F., (1991), *"Teacher stress leading to burnout: Its prevention and cure",* Education Today, 41 (2), pp. 12-16.

Maslach, C. (1982). "Understanding Burnout: Definitional issues in analysing a complex phenomenon." In W.S. Paine (Eds), *Job stress and burnout* (pp. 29-40). Bevrly Hills, CA: Sage.

Matheny, K. B., Gfroerer, C. A., & Harris, K. (2000). "Work stress, burnout, and coping at the turn of the century: An Adlerian perspective." *Journal of Individual Psychology, 56*(1), 74-87.

Pareek, U. (1982). *Role stress scale manual.* Ahmedabad, India: Navin Publication.

Pettersson, T., Postholm, M. B., Flem, A., and Gudmundsdottir, S. (2004). "The classroom as a stage and the teacher's role." *Teaching and Teacher Education, 20*, 589-605.

Raines, E.C. (2011). "A relational study of elementary principals' leadership traits, teacher morale, and school performance." *ProQuest LLC.*

Reddy, G.L., and Poornima, R., (2012), "Occupational Stress and Professional Burnout of University Teachers in South India", "International journal of Educational Planning and Administration." (2) pp. 109-124.

Reed, S. (1979). "What you can do to prevent teacher burnout." *National Elementary Principal, 58*(3), 67-70.

Richard, G. V., and Krieshok, T. S.,(1989), "Occupational stress, strain and coping strategies in university faculty", *Journal of Vocational Behaviour*, 34, pp.117-132.

Roloff, M.E., and Brown, L.A. (2011). "Extra-role time, burnout and commitment: the power of promises kept." *Business Communication Quarterly*, *74* (4), 450-474.

Sabel, R.H. and Sabel, M.K. (1982). "Factors in burnout among teachers of exceptional children." *Exceptional Children, 49*, 261-263.

Tims, M., Bakker, A. B., and Derks, D. (2013). "The impact of job crafting on job demands, job resources, and well-being." *Journal of Occupational Health Psychology, 18*, 230-240.

Trevers, C.J. and Copper, C.L. (1996). *Teachers under stress: Stress in teaching profession*. London: Routledge.

Tytherleigh, M. Y., Webb, C., Cooper, C. L., and Ricketts, C., (2005), "Occupational Stress in UK Higher Education Institutions: A Comparative Study of All Staff Categories", Higher Education Research and Development, 24 (1), February, pp. 41-61.

Valli, L., and Buese, D. (2007). "The changing roles of teachers in an era of high-stakes accountability." *American Educational Research Journal, 44*, 519-558.

22

Prospects and Practice of Adaptive Learning in India

Sutapa Das

Introduction

People, process and physical resources are three major components of a learning ecosystem. People includes learners, curriculum developers, educational administrators, instructional designers, curriculum evaluators, subject experts and teachers who develop, manage and implement various policies in educational field. In the process component, there are curriculum design and development, course delivery, proper transaction of curriculum in classroom environment, reception of feedback, construction of achievement test, evaluation of curriculum, training of teacher personnel and financial management for the improvement of the quality education. Physical resources refer to content and curriculum availability, study material, text books, classroom environment, paper-pencil based learning tools, institutional atmosphere, library, recreational facilities and playground accessibility of an educational institution. These three vital components are intricately acting with each other to make the learning ecosystem a functional one.

But, at present, in the pandemic situation caused by the widespread of COVID-19, the functionality of learning ecosystem will have been disrupted without the intervention of computer technology in the arena of education in India. This technological component which includes Learning Management System (LMS), learning record system, content management system, virtual teaching-learning system, mobile-based meeting platform and apps development system play a crucial role in present educational system. So, here with the forceful and needful introduction of technological component in the learning ecosystem, questions concerned with the adaptability to the new system are arising not only in the mind of learners but also all those who are involved in the field of education.

Again, if the concept of heterogeneity of learners is being considerably thought of, then, a changing model of teaching-learning must be essential. In conventional system, group of learners having different foundational knowledge and cognitive experience attend the same learning session and their varying level of emotional intelligence and competencies is mostly unattended and ignored much. Moreover, their level of comprehension, assimilation, approach of learning and skills of transferring knowledge are greatly influenced by their diverse educational, professional and personal experiences and learning preferences. Some learners like to listen lectures and ask questions while others prefer to use visual medium for their understanding along with listening or they like to behave in kinaesthetic way and engage themselves in doing some project works. From the techno-centric point of view, adaptive learning is highly preferable one to meet the needs of heterogeneous kind of learners by considering their individual preference of learning style and make them competent enough to use technology for academic purpose. So, adaptive learning forms a bridge between the Theory of Constructivism and application of Software Programming in teaching-learning environment.

Adaptive Learning

Adaptive Learning may be defined as "the process of generating a unique learning experience for each learner based on the learner's personality, interest and performance in order to achieve goals such as learner academic improvement, learner satisfaction, effective learning process and so forth."

It is the customisation of the design and delivery of learning based on each learner's individual learning needs and performance in real time. This approach is framed on research which shows that on exposure to same learning content, learners respond in different manner as they possess different levels of aptitudes, skills and orientations. Adaptive learning can recognise this diversity in learners and offer personalised self-regulating learning material.

Learners get customised content, self-assessment tools and immediate feedback, so that learners can gradually adapt themselves with the new learning material and build a mastery command on it which will enhance his application of knowledge by dynamic scaffolding. Data analysis techniques, algorithm-based learning models and artificial intelligence have made adaptive learning a reality for organisations.

Bases of Adaptive Learning

The source of adaptive is dual in nature, one is Constructivism and the other is Data Science. Constructivism is a theory of learning that has its root in both philosophy and psychology. The central theme of constructivism is that learners construct their knowledge by active introspection and analysis of experiences about their surroundings. They build a subjective type of knowledge which is not passively accumulated rather it is the result of active cognition by an individual. So, cognition is an adaptive process which prepares an individual to function and apply their acquired knowledge in a particular environment. The process of knowing has roots in neurological construction, social and cultural and language based interactions. Philosophically, also, the essence of constructivism relies on epistemology of subjectivism, relativism and experientialism.

Another aspect which supports adaptive learning is the scalable cloud-based big-data learning architecture. It includes a real-time or streaming layer, a standard-based protocol for describing, capturing and transmitting learning activities, short-term and long-term databases for persistent and transformed data, a parallelised computation layer and an output layer to support end-user visualisation.

Therefore, adaptive learning is a combination of active process of generation of knowledge through experience improvised by means of adaptation and artificial intelligence based large data learning architecture.

Important features of Adaptive Learning

In the learning ecosystem, the most important component is learner. So, every scientific research in the field of online learning is oriented towards learning process where learner's expectations, interest, motivation, learning styles, habits and demands are essentially taken into consideration. These factors highlight the essence of adaptive learning as an alternative to the traditional approach "one-sise-fits-all" in the development of teaching materials. The important features of adaptive learning are as follows:

- Adaptive learning is a comprehensive and complete blend of human brain and robotic brain where learner's behavior is tailored towards desirable direction by the help of artificial intelligence (AI) powered behavior of machine.
- It is totally self-regulatory learning system where learners can regulate their pace of learning according to their prior knowledge.
- Learners can make suitable correction in their responses by observing the feedback provided immediately by the system.
- It makes proper use of sensory organs of learners while learning process is going on.
- It encourages learners to take greater control and responsibility of their own learning by building a transparent open learner model.

- It is a generalised learning system which can be applied in any discipline from Science to Arts or Commerce.
- The flexible nature of this system can integrate virtual classroom with real classroom.
- It has the ability to assess the learner's characteristics and their learning preferences accurately and even their previous knowledge about the topic of discussion.
- It provides suitable feedback for proper reinforcement of learner's behavior which will enhance the level of motivation and interest in learning by reducing the level of difficulty and frustration of failure.
- It can be able to carry out quick decision and recommendations by identifying physical resources available at the moment of learning for proper understanding of the content.
- It can scale to support many users simultaneously during the process of learning.
- An important advantage of adaptive learning is that it helps an individual to reach the sone proximal development by dynamic scaffolding. Learner can identify the missing part in his behavior which creates a gap to reach the maximum level of his development.
- With the help of adaptive test, teachers can figure out the specific challenges that each individual faces and can work on those to iron out the problematic areas. Teachers can get the scope of doing necessary modification in their lesson plan and evaluation system.
- It is also cost-effective with respect to its maintenance and delivery.

Factors that Influence Adaptive learning

The successful function of adaptive learning depends on some essential factors which are:

1. *Learner* who is acting in the core of learning process has an influential effect on adaptive learning. His ability, choice, emotional behavior, level of motivation, level of understanding and also his skills of transferring technological knowledge in learning behavior influence the adaptive ability of learning. Mental health condition is another parameter which is noteworthy in learning process. Moreover, the number of learners is also a regulatory factor in adaptive learning.
2. *Teacher* who interacts with learners in the teaching-learning process in real classroom must be confident in using technology in learning and should create a virtual environment within the real classroom to motivate each and every learners in active participation. Teachers must be trained continuously through webinar, online workshop, conferences etc. with new innovations taking place in education system.
3. *Study disciplines* whether it is science or social science or literature based determine the function of adaptive learning.
4. *Infrastructure* which includes physical classroom, library, playground, conference hall of an institution is also a controlling factor in adaptive learning. They must be rearranged to receive the facility of adaptive learning by learners in maximum way.
5. *Evaluation* must be modified to assess individual level of understanding in a specific discipline and there must have the opportunity to select the method of evaluation by the learner. There will be choice of online along with offline mode of evaluation to neutralise the stress of examination faced by different learners.
6. *The government* also interferes in educational practices by implementing various educational policies time to time. Often this kind of policies have been determined by the ruling parties and there might be little consideration of future needs of the society.

Practice of Adaptive Learning in India

Implementing adaptive learning in India is not a simple task. When we are talking about Digital India, we must remember about to what extent the advancement of Information and Communication Technology could be successfully harnessed by common people living in rural and sub-urban corners of this country. The transformation of agriculture-based economic system of our country to a technology-based one is a matter of day dreaming. But, collaborating technology in every sector from business to education will give a meaningful standpoint in the economic as well as educational system in India. Application based knowledge and skills have been scarcely found in present youth generation and it is the real drawback in our present education system.

In conventional teaching-learning model, learners have always been exposed to a generalised curriculum which is not at all well-equipped with latest technology. Due to lack of suitable and sufficient amount of technology based infrastructural facilities and trained teachers, traditional method of teaching is still following in government schools. But in 21st century, globalisation and crisis in environment due to spread of COVID-19 are demanding a need of transformation in mode of learning. Parents in urban sectors are becoming much concerned about the future prospect of their children and their children are born and growing up in the realm of digital technology. Children become much more advanced in handling virtual reality than their parents, so, parents are trying to admit their children in schools improvised with modern teaching technology. Practicing adaptive learning by them is not a much difficult job under proper supervision of trained teachers. But, the real picture is that these private schools are demanding an increasing fees structure which is not always possible for guardians to afford.

On the other hand, in rural sectors, people realise the importance of technology in present day to day activities but their poor socio-economic status force them to accept their backwardness in all sectors. So, implementing individualised adaptive learning is just a luxury for them.

Conclusion

At present, conventional method of learning leads to poor academic performance among young learners in comparison to global development. Their intellect and abilities are highly challenged in global market. In this crucial juncture, adaptive learning is ensuring students to attend active learning by providing individualised and customised study material after assessing their previous knowledge about the topic of discussion. Moreover, the lesson plan is suitably fit for each and every learners and as per their learning styles. Hence the chance of becoming frustrated can be minimised and their level of motivation will automatically be increased. It can be said that adaptive learning is acting as a morale booster which helps to avail the quality education along with the quantitative expansion of knowledge. The need of wide-range of using technology in educational sector is knocking at the door. The present teaching-learning process in real classroom must be supplemented with computer-based adaptive learning to meet unique needs of each learner and to control different levels of learning difficulties by providing immediate feedback after each response. Learners can get the opportunity to be self-confident in responding independently and the skills they have developed can be applied in the workplace in proper way. But, challenges of high of implementation, inadequate support, need for training, inability to manage extensive amount of data are there in practicing adaptive learning. Implementing adaptive learning successfully in India requires time for creating detailed revision of curriculum and content that supports learning objectives and initiative by government to make easy access of technology by common people living in the remotest corner of this country.

References

Charles, et.al. *Adaptive learning in Psychology: Wayfinding in the Digital Age,* Online Learning, Sept., 2016, Vol. 20 (3).

Ennovamani, S., and Mahani, S. *An Overview of adaptive e-learning systems,* Research Gate, Dec, 2017. https://www.researchgate.net/publication/322586183.

Essa, A. "A possible future for next generation adaptive learning systems," *Smart learning Environments,* 2016.

Gwyn, et.al. "Adaptive Learning: An Innovative Method for Online Teaching and Learning," *Journal of Extension,* Sep., 2018, Vol. 56 (5).

Khalid, et.al. "A Survey of Artificial Intelligence Techniques employed for Adaptive Educational Systems within E-learning platforms." *JAISCR,* 2017, Vol. 7(1), pp. 47-64.

Khosravi, H., Sadiq, S., and Gasevic, D. "Development and Adoption of an Adaptive Learning System," In the Proceeding of The 51st ACM *Technical Symposium on Computer Science Education,* Portland, OR, USA, Mar. 11-14, 2020. https://doi.org/10.1145/332877866900.

Matei, A., and Gogu, M.C., "Adaptive Education – A Systematic view, Proceedings of EDULEARN17 Conference," 3rd-5th July, 2017, Barcelona, Spain. https://www.researchgate.net/publication/318705604.

Radhan, B. D., *Adaptive Learning: A Cost-Effective Alternative to Tuitions in India,* Higher Education Digest, June, 25, 2019.

Sarmanova, J., and Kostolanyova, K., "Adaptive E-learning: From Theory to Practice," *ICTE Journal,* 2015, Vol.4(4), pp. 34-47.

23

A Study on Consequences of Digital Education on Learners with Mental Retardation during the COVID-19 Pandemic

Utsa Bhattacharjee and **Saheli Saha**

Introduction

Digital learning is also referred to as e-learning or technology-enhanced learning, is accompanied by technology and use digital tools during teaching learning practices. It encompasses the application of a wide range of learning practices including virtual and blended learning. On the other hand, differently abled learners are those who learn differently or take more time to learn compare to non-disabled learners. This study has emphasised on the learning process of differently abled learners during the pandemic with a special reference of learners with mental retardation. The American Association on Mental Deficiency (AAMD) defined Mental Retardation as a significantly sub-average general intellectual functioning resulting in or associated with concurrent impairments in adaptive behaviour and manifested during the developmental period. The Census 2011 showed that in India, about 2.68 crore people are disabled which is 2.21 percent of the total population. It also informed that 61 percent of the disabled children aged 5-19 years are attending educational institutions. Nevertheless, MHRD initiates online education due to COVID-19 pandemic so that learner's educational process doesn't get hampered. In this way,

India's education model and regular classes suddenly shifted to the digital modes without considering disabled learners as school education of special children has always been at a crossroads. Differently abled learners especially the mentally retarded ones cannot easily access digital tools because most of the digital contents are not in an accessible format for disable people. In this way the digital divide is formed gradually between differently abled learners and non-disabled learners.

Purpose of the Study

The research objectives are as follows –

- To examine how much online classes are beneficial for differently abled learners specially the mentally retarded one during the pandemic.
- To analyse the role of teachers as well as parents in case of teaching differently abled learners during the lockdown period.
- To find out important measures what may take to ensure equality and equity on the virtual platform.

Review of Related Literature

According to a study conducted by United Nations Educational, Scientific, and Cultural Organisation, it has been identified that speedy development of the era of information and communication technology (ICT) brings possibilities as well as dangers to the people with special needs. Mostly the principal information on the digital platform is presented in a way that children with special needs are excluded from its access. Moreover, the digital divide, on its own, had intensified social exclusion. Bheemeshwar Reddy A (2020) stated that the decision to launch massive online education had taken without the participation of important stakeholders in the education system namely students, teachers and parents. Government of India neglected some vital factors that some disadvantaged students may not have digital infrastructure such as poor, special children, students from rural areas and so on. On the other hand, Pratt (1999) stated that worldwide special educators realised the importance of technology to teach students with special needs in regular as well as special classrooms. According to Kamei-Hannan (2008), CAT (Computerised Adapted Testing) is considered one of the assistive technologies being used in educational areas to measure progress and accountability.

Methodology

The main focus of Qualitative research methods is to provide a complete picture of the scenario with a detailed analysis of inter-relation. This study is mainly based on primary and secondary data. For this study, five teachers of 'Amrit Somani Memorial Centre – Behavioural Intervention' including an equal number of parents of mentally retarded children were interviewed. Secondary data have been collected from a large resource of written material including books, academic journals, news articles, as well as official websites of national and international organisations.

Theoretical aspect

Digital divide, the term was introduced in the mid-1990s. It describes the fact that the world can be divided into two kinds of people, the one who has access and capability to use modern information technology (IT) and those who don't have the digital infrastructure or have restricted access. Spectar (2000) stated that the internet itself is seen as the two-faced role in the diving process as it has the potentiality to increase or decrease the gap between rich and poor worldwide. During the 1970s the third world countries started to demand an immediate restructuration of the international economic, information and communication orders. In this circumstance, the MAcBridge Commission presented a preliminary report at the 20th General Conference of UNESCO in Paris in the year 1978. The MacBridge commission is also known as Many Voices one World, it echoed the views of the developing countries regarding global communication policies and emphasised on the free and balanced flow of information to decrease information gap. Still, there are a large number of people especially from developing countries who cannot access modern technology due to poverty, disabilities and many other reasons. According to Singh (2010), the digital divide has many dimensions and it is categorised as global, national and regional. There are multiple divides at the national level: for instance between men and women, rich and poor, young and elderly, rural and urban etc. But most people forget about the digital divide between disabled and non-disabled individuals.

Lindsay (2010) informed that disability is often an overlooked aspect of the digital divide and it should be taken into sincerely when we talk about digital inequality. Information and communication technology become more accessible for disabled people as it provides information, rehabilitation and an opportunity for social inclusion. In India, about sixty million individuals are disabled and seventy five percent of them are from rural areas where digital infrastructure is hardly available. India is also a participant to both Biwako Millennium framework (2002) and UNCRPD (2006) towards a barrier-free, inclusive and rights-based society for persons with disabilities in Asia and Pacific. Persons with Disabilities Act (1995) also ensure full participation in society and equality of disabled persons. Whereas there is no specific legalisation which ensures the right of disabled people to access in ICTs.

Findings of the Study

Primary data analysis

Usually, every child with special needs has an individualised educational plan which is specially made for them, but during the pandemic special educators of 'Amrit Somani Memorial Centre – Behavioural Intervention' could not maintain these plans over online classes. Teachers of this special school have told us that they tried to teach their special students over phone or laptop but they cannot succeed as sending notes and assignments via WhatsApp or email is not helpful for learners with special needs. Besides most of the parents are used to depend on special educators regarding their special child's education. But due to the lockdown time, special educators could not visit their homes and parents have to struggle way more than they should. Due to lack of knowledge parents were not able to teach them properly and their kids were getting frustrated. It had been identified that the process of motivating a special child to learn something, required a lot of time, patience including experience and it is totally based on their present condition which is not understandable to all the parents. Then teachers shared children's individualised educational plan with their parents respectively and teach them how to follow it. After that parents started to record their child's learning video and shared it with the special educators. However, teachers analysed those videos and guided parents accordingly but they could not understand the child's present mood and help them efficiently. In this way, the school authority had continued their learning program but they all knew that it is not the right way to teach a special child. Differently abled children always want more care and patience which is not possible to provide over WhatsApp or email videos.

Secondary Data Analysis

According to the report of National Sample Survey Office (NSSO) on social consumption of education (2017-18) informs that in India only nine percent of students who are currently enrolled in any course have access to basic digital infrastructure, which means that over ninety one percent of students are left behind from having access. Therefore the attempt to make online education an opportunity to deal with COVID-19 crisis raises a serious risk towards many learners, especially for the disabled learners and socio-economically disadvantaged learners. On the other hand, article 9 states that Persons with Disabilities have the right to access information, communication and technology (ICT) systems. Besides Section 42 of the Rights of Persons with Disabilities Act, 2016 directs the government to ensure that all contents which are available in audio, print and electronic media should be in an accessible format so that all citisens can access them easily. Meanwhile, it is a compulsory domestic legal obligation to ensure accessibility of digital education system both from the perspective of design and infrastructure. The Right to Education Act (2009) ensured norms and standards only for physical infrastructure. The Act states that teaching and learning equipment will be provided to each class without considering digitalised equipment facilities that must be inclusive also.

In order to ensure access Education through online platforms, the Ministry of Human Resource Development (MHRD) initiates platforms like e-Pathshala, e-Vidya, SWAYAM, Digital Infrastructure for Knowledge Sharing (DIKSHA) etc. A recent press released by MHRD revealed that the lockdown period had witnessed vast participation in online platforms like SWAYAM and other digital initiatives. But there were no mentions of how many of these beneficiaries are special learners or how these platforms are being suited to meet their needs. Recently the Department of Empowerment of Persons with Disability, under the Ministry of Social Justice and Welfare has released guidelines for essential protection and safety of persons with disabilities during COVID-19 CRISIS, which ensured some essential services and assistance to persons with disabilities, but the government did not take account the educational needs of differently abled learners. However, the NPE 2020 aligns with the objectives of the Rights of Persons with Disabilities (PWD) Act 2016. The policy aims to recruit special educators in all schools to ensure more inclusiveness, home schooling will also be allowed to the learners with benchmark disabilities. All the teachers will be trained to identify disabilities among learners in early-stage and take care of their mental health. In order to ensure equitability in the assessment procedure, National Assessment Center PARAKH will also be formulated under this policy. However, NPE 2020 did not recognise the fact many teachers are poorly trained and most of the Indian schools are grossly understaffed. A recent evaluation was undertaken by the Delhi Child Rights commission shown that sixty percent of schools reported sero students with disabilities and twenty eight percent reported less than one percent. So it is quite clear that reality is far more different compare to government initiative.

Conclusion

It is concluded that there is a lack of awareness among parents, they face a continuous barrage of challenges from societal isolation, face difficulties to find proper resources to teach their special children. Besides, there are lacks of infrastructure, monetary help from the government including special educators. Online classrooms in India were already outdated and COVID-19 just made it worse. Education for differently abled learners has mostly been seen from the point of access rather than inclusion, but this pandemic is an opportunity to change that view. However, the sudden shift to digital mode of regular classes has increased the digital divide between a disabled child and a non-disabled one. Government initiatives are not enough, there must be awareness programs and workshops to ensure the success of such government policies.

Suggestion

Here are some suggestion to ensure equality and equity in online classes

- The Ministry of Human Resource Development should coordinate with the Department of Empowerment of Persons with Disabilities as well as the Ministry of Electronics and IT to formulate standardised guidelines for digital education infrastructure for learners with special needs as per the Rights of Persons with Disabilities Act. In addition these guidelines should be mandatory for all ICT providers like public and private education organisation.
- In order to develop comprehensive guidelines regarding the accessibility of virtual education the National policy on ICT in School Education needs to review and update based on some specific Acts and Policies. It is also important to reschedule the RTE Act to include norms and standards on inclusive digital education which will apply to schools.
- School authority can arrange some interaction sessions to teach parents how to cope up with their special child

without taking the help of special educators. In addition they may also organise to educate parents about the uses of software techniques that assist differently abled pupils. There are some applications of Assistive Technology in E-learning such as scanning software, independent text reading, text telephone (TTY), augmentative and alternative communication (AAC), abbreviation expanders etc.

Moreover, there must be some willingness and sincerity in our society regarding the education of special children otherwise no government policy can change people's age-old mindset. Universal accessibility norms must be an integral part of the content creation process rather than a supplementary implementation.

References

A, B. R. (2020, September 05). "Of Access and Inclusivity." *Economic and Political weekly*, p. 36.

Kamei-Hannan, C. (2008). "Examining the accessibility of a computerised adapted test using assistive technology." *Journal of Visual Impairment &Blindness*, 261-271.

Lindsay, S. (2010). *Disability and the digital divide: gaps and future directions.* Internet Issues: Blogging, Digital Divide and Digital Libraries. New York, NY: Nova Science Publishers.

Pratt, B. (1999). "Making it work: Using technology in a classroom for young children with multiple disabilities." *Learning and Leading with Technology*, 28-31.

Singh, S. (2010). "Digital divide in India: Measurement, determinants and policy for addressing the challenges in bridging the digital divide." *International Journal of Innovation in the Digital Economy* (IJIDE), 1-24.

Spectar, J. (2000). "Bridging the Global Digital Divide: Frameworks for Access and the World Wireless Web." *North Carolina Journal of International Law*, 26-57.

https://iite.unesco.org/pics/publications/en/files/3214644.pdf

http://www.rehabcouncil.nic.in/writereaddata/mr.pdf

http://mospi.nic.in/sites/default/files/publication_reports/Disabled_persons_in_India_2016.pdf

http://www.mospi.gov.in/sites/default/files/NSS75252E/KI_Education_75th_Final.pdf

https://www.epw.in/journal/2020/36/commentary/access-and-inclusivity.html

https://theprint.in/opinion/indias-online-classrooms-are-outdated-for-disabled-kids-covid-just-made-it-worse/463438/

The Contributors

1. **Abhishek Das,** Assistant Professor, Department of English, Alipurduar Mahila Mahavidyalaya, email: abhishek.das66@gmail.com
2. **Dr. Ajay Prakash Tiwari,** Assistant Professor, Department of Education, C. M. P. College (Prayagraj), email: ajaytiwari.alld@gmail.com
3. **Dr. Dileep Kumar Maurya,** M. Ed, M. Phil, Ph.D
4. **Dr. Aniruddha Burmon,** Associate Professor, Department of English, University B.T. & Evening College, Cooch Behar, email: aburmon@gmail.com
5. **Bhaskar Chaudhuri,** Associate Professor, Department of Geography, Bijoy Krishna Girls' College, email: bhaskarchowdhuri122@gmail.com
6. **Bidushi Saha**, State Aided College Teacher, Department of English, Alipurduar Mahila Mahavidyalaya, email: bidushisaha266@gmail.com
7. **Bitasta Goswami,** Assistant Professor, Department of Political Science, Alipurduar Mahila Mahavidyalaya, email: email: bitasta88@gmail.com
8. **Boni Dutta**, Assistant Professor, Department of History, Alipurduar Mahila Mahavidyalaya, email: deb.bonidutta@gmail.com
9. **Indranil Ghosh,** M. Sc., M. Ed., email: indranil1992ghosh@gmail.com
10. **Jayeeta Roy,** Assistant Professor, Department of Philosophy, Alipurduar Mahila Mahavidyalaya, email: jayeetaroy99@gmail.com
11. **Joydeep Singh,** Assistant professor, Department of History, Alipurduar Mahila Mahavidyalaya, email: joydeeps447@gmail.com
12. **Nabanita Dutta,** Assistant Professor, Department of Education, Panskura Banamali College, email: duttanabanita1@gmail.com

13. **Namit Lepcha,** Assistant Professor, Department of Political Science, Alipurduar Mahila Mahavidyalaya, email: sarannamit@gmail.com

14. **P. Ravi Kumar,** Research Scholar, Department of Educational Psychology, Tamil Nadu Teacher's Education University, email: sendsvet@gmail.com

15. **Dr. P.N. Lakshmi Sghanmugam,** Assistant Professor, Department of Educational Psychology, Tamil Nadu Teacher's Education University, email: pnlsnnm@gmail.com

16. **Poulomi Modak,** Junior Research Fellow, Department of English, Cooch Behar Panchanan Barma University, email: poulomimodak1992@gmail.com

17. **Dr. Prasanta Kumar Barik,** Assistant Professor, Department of Education, Rajiv Gandhi University, email: prasantabarik77@gmail.com

18. **Dr. Priyanka Bose Das,** Assistant Professor, Department of Education, Budge Budge College, email: bosepriyanka.bose006@gmail.com

19. **Dr. Ritwika Laskar,** Assistant Professor, Department of Education, Alipurduar Mahila Mahavidyalaya, email: ritwikalaskar@gmail.com

20. **Saheli Saha**, State Aided College Teacher, Department of Education, Alipurduar Mahila Mahavidyalaya, email: sahelisaha1029@gmail.com

21. **Dr. Srabanti Mukhopadhyay,** Assistant Professor (Stage 3), Department of Education, Gokhale Memorial Girls' College, email: srabanti2018@rediffmail.com

22. **Sumita Chatterjee,** Assistant Professor, Department of Education, Bamanpukur Humayun Kabir Mahavidyalaya, email: sumichatu@gmail.com

23. **Sushant Kumar Nayak,** Assistant Professor, Department of Education, Rajiv Gandhi University, email: Sushant.k.nayak@gmail.com

24. **Sutapa Das**, Assistant Professor, Department of Education, Alipurduar Mahila Mahavidyalaya, email: ammsutapa@gmail.com

25. **Utsa Bhattacharjee,** State Aided College Teacher, Department of Journalism and Mass Communication, Hiralal Masumdar Memorial College for Women, email: utsabhattacharjee.84@gmail.com

Index

R

S

T

U

V

W